MIX

THE AUSTRALIAN
Women's Weekly

MIX

cakes, muffins, biscuits + puddings

acp
books

contents

Scones need a light touch, a cool kitchen and cold hands. The quicker you are at mixing the liquid into the dry ingredients, the lighter your scones. For soft scones, cook them in a cake pan; for crunchy scones, use an oven tray.

Muffins become stodgy when the mixture is overhandled. Barely mix the liquid into the dry ingredients for really light muffins, taking no notice of lumps.

Friands are quick and simple to make – even a child can make friands – and they're at their best if eaten on the day they're made.

Cakes, both big and small, should be mixed with electric beaters, not a blender or food processor. Start with the beaters

on low speed and once the mixture is
combined, increase the speed to medium.
Biscuits will have the right shape and
texture if the mixture is not overbeaten.
To test if a biscuit is cooked, push it gently
with your finger while it is still on the oven
tray – if it moves without breaking, the
biscuit is cooked.
Slices usually feel slightly soft when they
first come out of the oven. Most recipes
call for them to be cooled in the pan before
being cut into squares or rectangles.
Puddings that are baked or steamed are
generally extremely easy to make – not
a lot of preparation is required, but they
sometimes take a while to cook.

scones

Basic scones

2½ cups (375g) self-raising flour
1 tablespoon caster sugar
30g butter
¾ cup (180ml) milk
½ cup (125ml) water, approximately

1 Preheat oven to 220°C/200°C fan-forced. Grease deep 19cm-square cake pan.
2 Sift flour and sugar into large bowl; rub in butter with fingertips.
3 Make well in centre of flour mixture; add milk and almost all of the water. Using a knife, "cut" the milk and water through the flour mixture to mix to a soft, sticky dough. Knead dough on floured surface until smooth.
4 Press dough out to a 2cm thickness. Dip 4.5cm cutter into flour; cut as many rounds as you can from the piece of dough. Place scones side by side, just touching, in pan. Gently knead scraps of dough together; repeat pressing and cutting of dough. Place in same pan. Brush tops with a little extra milk.
5 Bake scones about 15 minutes or until browned and scones sound hollow when tapped firmly on the top with fingers.

preparation time 20 minutes
cooking time 15 minutes **makes** 16
tip When a recipes says "cut" the liquid through the dry ingredients, it means don't stir, just use a knife quickly and lightly to draw the knife through the flour, so moistening the dry ingredients as lightly as possible. This is done to prevent overworking the flour which causes tough scones.

Pumpkin scones

You will need to cook about 250g pumpkin for this recipe.

40g butter, softened
¼ cup (55g) caster sugar
1 egg
¾ cup cooked mashed pumpkin
2½ cups (375g) self-raising flour
½ teaspoon ground nutmeg
⅓ cup (80ml) milk, approximately

1 Preheat oven to 220°C/200°C fan-forced. Grease two 20cm-round sandwich pans or oven tray.
2 Beat butter, sugar and egg in small bowl with electric mixer until light and fluffy. Transfer mixture to large bowl. Stir in pumpkin, then sifted dry ingredients and enough milk to make a soft, sticky dough. Knead dough on floured surface until smooth.
3 Press dough out to a 2cm thickness. Dip 5cm cutter into flour; cut as many rounds as you can from the piece of dough. Place scones side by side, just touching, in pan. Gently knead scraps of dough together; repeat pressing and cutting of dough. Place in same pan. Brush tops with a little extra milk.
4 Bake scones about 15 minutes or until browned and scones sound hollow when tapped firmly on the top with fingers.

preparation time 20 minutes
cooking time 15 minutes **makes** 20

Sultana and lemon scones

2½ cups (375g) self-raising flour
1 tablespoon caster sugar
30g butter
½ cup (80g) sultanas
2 teaspoons grated lemon rind
¾ cup (180ml) milk
½ cup (125ml) water, approximately

1 Preheat oven to 220°C/200°C fan-forced. Grease deep 19cm-square cake pan.
2 Sift flour and sugar into large bowl; rub in butter with fingertips. Stir in sultanas and rind.
3 Make well in centre of flour mixture; add milk and almost all of the water. Using a knife, "cut" the milk and water through the flour mixture to mix to a soft, sticky dough. Knead dough on floured surface until smooth.
4 Press dough out to a 2cm thickness. Dip 4.5cm cutter into flour; cut as many rounds as you can from the piece of dough. Place scones side by side, just touching, in pan. Gently knead scraps of dough together; repeat pressing and cutting of dough. Place in same pan. Brush tops with a little extra milk.
5 Bake scones about 15 minutes or until browned and scones sound hollow when tapped firmly on the top with fingers.

preparation time 25 minutes
cooking time 15 minutes **makes** 16

Date scones

2 cups (300g) self-raising flour
2 teaspoons caster sugar
15g butter
1 cup (160g) finely chopped seeded dried dates
1 cup (250ml) milk, approximately

1 Preheat oven to 240°C/220°C fan-forced. Grease 20cm-round sandwich pan or oven tray.
2 Sift flour and sugar into medium bowl; rub in butter with fingertips. Stir in dates.
3 Make well in centre of flour mixture; add milk. Using a knife, "cut" the milk through the flour mixture to mix to a soft, sticky dough. Knead dough on floured surface until smooth.
4 Press dough out evenly to 2cm thickness. Dip 5cm cutter into as many rounds as you can from piece of dough. Place scones side by side, just touching, in pan. Brush tops with a little extra milk.
5 Bake scones about 15 minutes or until browned and scones sound hollow when tapped firmly on the top with fingers.

variation
wholemeal scones Omit dates. Replace the self-raising flour with 1 cup (160g) wholemeal self-raising flour and 1 cup (150g) white self-raising flour.

preparation time 20 minutes
cooking time 15 minutes **makes** 10

Cardamom marmalade scones

2½ cups (375g) self-raising flour
1 tablespoon caster sugar
30g butter
1 teaspoon ground cardamom
2 teaspoons finely grated orange rind
1 cup (250ml) milk
⅓ cup (115g) orange marmalade

1 Preheat oven to 220°C/200°C fan-forced. Grease deep 19cm-square cake pan.
2 Sift flour and sugar into large bowl; rub in butter with fingertips. Stir in cardamom and rind.
3 Make well in centre of flour mixture; add combined milk and marmalade. Using a knife, "cut" the milk and marmalade through the flour mixture to mix to a soft, sticky dough. Knead dough on floured surface until smooth.
4 Press dough out to a 2cm thickness. Dip 4.5cm cutter into flour; cut as many rounds as you can from the piece of dough. Place scones side by side, just touching, in pan. Gently knead scraps of dough together; repeat pressing and cutting of dough. Place in same pan. Brush tops with a little extra milk.
5 Bake scones about 15 minutes or until browned and scones sound hollow when tapped firmly on the top with fingers.

preparation time 25 minutes
cooking time 15 minutes **makes** 16

Blueberry ginger scones

2½ cups (375g) self-raising flour
1 tablespoon caster sugar
30g butter
3 teaspoons ground ginger
½ cup (75g) fresh or frozen blueberries
¾ cup (180ml) milk
½ cup (125ml) water, approximately

1 Preheat oven to 220°C/200°C fan-forced. Grease deep 19cm-square cake pan.
2 Sift flour and sugar into large bowl; rub in butter with fingertips. Stir in ginger and blueberries.
3 Make well in centre of flour mixture; add milk and almost all of the water. Using a knife, "cut" the milk and water through the flour mixture to mix to a soft, sticky dough. Knead dough on floured surface until smooth.
4 Press dough out to a 2cm thickness. Dip 4.5cm cutter into flour; cut as many rounds as you can from the piece of dough. Place scones side by side, just touching, in pan. Gently knead scraps of dough together; repeat pressing and cutting of dough. Place in same pan. Brush tops with a little extra milk.
5 Bake scones about 15 minutes or until browned and scones sound hollow when tapped firmly on the top with fingers.

preparation time 25 minutes
cooking time 15 minutes **makes** 16

Caramel apple pull-apart

2 cups (300g) self-raising flour
30g butter
1 cup (250ml) milk, approximately
⅓ cup (65g) firmly packed brown sugar
400g can pie apples
pinch ground nutmeg
½ teaspoon ground cinnamon
2 tablespoons coarsely chopped toasted pecans
caramel
¼ cup (60ml) cream
20g butter
½ cup (100g) firmly packed brown sugar

1 Preheat oven to 200°C/180°C fan-forced. Grease deep 22cm-round cake pan.
2 Sift flour into medium bowl; rub in butter with fingertips.
3 Make a well in centre of flour mixture; add enough milk to mix to a soft, sticky dough. Knead dough on floured surface until smooth.
4 Roll dough on floured baking paper to 21cm x 40cm rectangle. Sprinkle dough with sugar, spread with combined apples and spices to within 3cm from long edge. Using paper as a guide, roll dough up like a swiss roll, from long side. Use a floured, serrated knife to cut roll into 12 slices. Place 11 slices upright around edge of pan; place remaining slice in centre.
5 Bake pull-apart about 25 minutes. Stand a few minutes before turning onto wire rack.
6 Meanwhile, make caramel.
7 Brush hot pull-apart evenly with caramel, sprinkle with nuts.
caramel Stir ingredients in small saucepan constantly over heat, without boiling, until sugar is dissolved. Simmer, uncovered, without stirring, about 3 minutes or until mixture is thickened slightly.

preparation time 35 minutes
cooking time 25 minutes **makes** 12

Spicy fruit scones

1¼ cups (310ml) hot strong strained black tea
¾ cup (135g) mixed dried fruit
3 cups (450g) self-raising flour
1 teaspoon ground cinnamon
1 teaspoon mixed spice
2 tablespoons caster sugar
20g butter
½ cup (120g) sour cream, approximately

1 Preheat oven to 220°C/200°C fan-forced. Grease 23cm-square slab cake pan.
2 Combine tea and fruit in small heatproof bowl, cover, stand 20 minutes or until mixture is cooled to room temperature.
3 Sift dry ingredients into large bowl; rub in butter with fingertips. Stir in fruit mixture and enough sour cream to mix to a soft, sticky dough. Knead dough on floured surface until smooth.
4 Press dough out evenly to 2cm thickness. Dip 5.5cm cutter into flour; cut as many rounds as you can from piece of dough. Place scones side by side, just touching, in pan. Gently knead scraps of dough together; repeat pressing and cutting out of dough, place in same pan. Brush tops with a little milk
5 Bake scones about 15 minutes or until browned and scones sound hollow when tapped firmly on the top with fingers.

preparation time 20 minutes (plus standing time)
cooking time 15 minutes **makes** 16

Buttermilk scones
with strawberries and cream

3 cups (450g) self-raising flour
2 tablespoons caster sugar
40g butter
2 cups (500ml) buttermilk
2 tablespoons buttermilk, extra
300ml thickened cream
250g strawberries, halved

1 Preheat oven to 240°C/220°C fan-forced. Grease 20cm x 30cm lamington pan.
2 Sift flour and sugar into large bowl; rub in butter with fingertips.
3 Make well in centre of flour mixture; add buttermilk. Using a knife, "cut" the buttermilk through the flour mixture to mix to a soft, sticky dough. Knead dough on floured surface until smooth.
4 Press dough out to 2.5cm thickness. Dip 6.5cm cutter into flour; cut as many rounds as possible from the piece of dough. Place scones side by side, just touching, in pan. Gently knead scraps of dough together; repeat pressing and cutting out of dough. Place in pan. Brush tops with extra buttermilk.
5 Bake scones about 20 minutes or until browned and scones sound hollow when tapped firmly on the top with fingers.
6 Meanwhile, beat cream in small bowl with electric mixer until soft peaks form. Serve scones with whipped cream and strawberries.

preparation time 20 minutes
cooking time 20 minutes **makes** 15

Honey and muesli scones

2½ cups (375g) self-raising flour
1 teaspoon ground cinnamon
1 tablespoon caster sugar
30g butter
½ cup (65g) toasted muesli
¼ cup (90g) honey
¾ cup (180ml) milk

1 Preheat oven to 220°C/200°C fan-forced. Grease deep 19cm-square cake pan.
2 Sift flour, cinnamon and sugar into large bowl; rub in butter with fingertips. Add muesli.
3 Make well in centre of flour mixture; add honey and milk. Using a knife, "cut" the honey and milk through the flour mixture to mix to a soft, sticky dough. Knead dough on floured surface until smooth.
4 Press dough out to a 2cm thickness. Dip 4.5cm cutter into flour; cut as many rounds as you can from the piece of dough. Place scones side by side, just touching, in pan. Gently knead scraps of dough together; repeat pressing and cutting of dough. Place in same pan. Brush tops with a little extra milk.
5 Bake scones about 15 minutes or until browned and scones sound hollow when tapped firmly on the top with fingers.

preparation time 25 minutes
cooking time 15 minutes **makes** 16

Butterscotch curls

60g butter, softened
⅓ cup (75g) firmly packed brown sugar
¼ cup (30g) chopped walnuts
3 cups (450g) self-raising flour
90g butter, extra
1¼ cups (310ml) milk, approximately
⅓ cup (75g) firmly packed brown sugar, extra

1 Preheat oven to 200°C/180°C fan-forced. Grease deep 20cm-round cake pan.
2 Beat butter and sugar in small bowl with wooden spoon until just combined. Spread butter mixture over base of pan; sprinkle with nuts.
3 Sift flour into medium bowl; rub in half of the extra butter with fingertips. Add enough milk to mix to a firm dough. Knead gently on floured surface until smooth. Roll dough to 23cm x 28cm rectangle.
4 Melt remaining extra butter, brush over dough, sprinkle with extra sugar. Roll dough up like a swiss roll, from long side. Cut into 10 rounds, place cut-side up in pan.
5 Bake curls about 25 minutes.

preparation time 40 minutes
cooking time 25 minutes **makes** 10 curls

Apricot and almond scones

2½ cups (375g) self-raising flour
1 tablespoon caster sugar
30g butter
1 teaspoon mixed spice
1 cup (150g) finely chopped dried apricots
⅓ cup (45g) finely chopped roasted slivered almonds
¾ cup (180ml) milk
½ cup (125ml) water, approximately

1 Preheat oven to 220°C/200°C fan-forced. Grease deep 19cm-square cake pan.
2 Sift flour and sugar into large bowl; rub in butter with fingertips. Stir in spice, apricots and nuts.
3 Make well in centre of flour mixture; add milk and almost all of the water. Using a knife, "cut" the milk and water through the flour mixture to mix to a soft, sticky dough. Knead dough on floured surface until smooth.
4 Press dough out to a 2cm thickness. Dip 4.5cm cutter into flour; cut as many rounds as you can from the piece of dough. Place scones side by side, just touching, in pan. Gently knead scraps of dough together; repeat pressing and cutting of dough. Place in same pan. Brush tops with a little extra milk.
5 Bake scones about 15 minutes or until browned and scones sound hollow when tapped firmly on the top with fingers.

preparation time 25 minutes
cooking time 15 minutes **makes** 16

muffins

Berry yogurt muffins

We used a mixture of raspberries and blueberries in these muffins.

1½ cups (225g) self-raising flour
⅓ cup (30g) rolled oats
3 eggs
¾ cup (165g) firmly packed brown sugar
¾ cup (200g) yogurt
⅓ cup (80ml) vegetable oil
180g fresh or frozen berries

1 Preheat oven to 200°C/180°C fan-forced. Grease 6-hole texas (¾-cup/180ml) muffin pan.
2 Combine sifted flour with oats in medium bowl; stir in eggs, sugar, yogurt and oil. Do not over-mix; mixture should be lumpy. Gently stir in berries. Spoon mixture into pan holes.
3 Bake muffins about 20 minutes. Stand in pan 5 minutes before turning onto wire rack.

preparation time 10 minutes
cooking time 20 minutes **makes** 6

Berry muffins

2½ cups (375g) self-raising flour
90g cold butter, chopped
1 cup (220g) caster sugar
1¼ cups (310ml) buttermilk
1 egg, beaten lightly
200g fresh or frozen mixed berries

1 Preheat oven to 180°C/160°C fan-forced. Grease 12-hole
(⅓-cup/80ml) muffin pan.
2 Sift flour into large bowl; rub in butter with fingertips. Stir in sugar,
buttermilk and egg. Do not over-mix; mixture should be lumpy. Gently
stir in berries. Spoon mixture into pan holes.
3 Bake muffins about 20 minutes. Stand in pan 5 minutes before
turning onto wire rack.

variations
lemon poppy seed
Omit berries. Add 2 teaspoons lemon rind and 2 tablespoons poppy
seeds with the sugar.
date and orange
Omit berries. Substitute self-raising flour with 1 cup wholemeal self-raising
flour and 1½ cups white self-raising flour. Add 1½ cups chopped dried
dates and 2 teaspoons finely grated orange rind with the sugar.
choc chip and walnut
Omit berries. Add ¾ cup dark Choc Bits and 1 cup coarsely chopped
walnuts with the sugar.

preparation time 10 minutes
cooking time 20 minutes **makes** 12
tip Muffins can be stored in an airtight container for up to 2 days or
frozen for up to 2 months.

Banana maple muffins

You will need about 2 small overripe bananas (260g) for this recipe.

2 cups (300g) self-raising flour
⅓ cup (50g) plain flour
½ teaspoon bicarbonate of soda
½ cup (110g) firmly packed brown sugar
¼ cup (60ml) maple-flavoured syrup
⅔ cup mashed banana
2 eggs, beaten lightly
1 cup (250ml) buttermilk
⅓ cup (80ml) vegetable oil
coconut topping
15g butter
1 tablespoon maple-flavoured syrup
⅔ cup (30g) flaked coconut

1 Preheat oven to 200°C/180°C fan-forced. Grease 12-hole
(⅓-cup/80ml) muffin pan.
2 Make coconut topping.
3 Sift dry ingredients into large bowl. Stir in maple syrup and banana,
then egg, buttermilk and oil. Do not over-mix; mixture should be lumpy.
Spoon mixture into pan holes; sprinkle with coconut topping.
4 Bake muffins about 20 minutes. Stand in pan 5 minutes before
turning onto wire rack.
coconut topping Melt butter in small saucepan, add maple syrup and
coconut; stir constantly over high heat until coconut is browned lightly.
Remove from heat.

preparation time 15 minutes
cooking time 25 minutes **makes** 12
tip Serve with crispy bacon for a scrumptious brunch with a difference.

Choc brownie muffins

2 cups (300g) self-raising flour
⅓ cup (35g) cocoa powder
⅓ cup (75g) caster sugar
60g butter, melted
½ cup (95g) Choc Bits
½ cup (75g) pistachios, chopped coarsely
½ cup (165g) chocolate hazelnut spread
1 egg, beaten lightly
¾ cup (180ml) milk
½ cup (120g) sour cream

1 Preheat oven to 200°C/180°C fan-forced. Grease 12-hole
(⅓-cup/80ml) muffin pan.
2 Sift dry ingredients into large bowl; stir in remaining ingredients.
Do not over-mix; mixture should be lumpy. Spoon mixture into pan holes.
3 Bake muffins about 20 minutes. Stand in pan 5 minutes before
turning onto wire rack. Dust with sifted extra cocoa, if you like.

preparation time 15 minutes
cooking time 20 minutes **makes** 12
tip Take care not to overcook these little indulgences – they should be
slightly moist in the middle.

Ginger date muffins with caramel sauce

1 cup (160g) chopped seeded dried dates
⅓ cup (80ml) water
¼ teaspoon bicarbonate of soda
2 cups (300g) self-raising flour
1 cup (150g) plain flour
2 teaspoons ground ginger
½ teaspoon mixed spice
1 cup (220g) firmly packed brown sugar
2 teaspoons grated orange rind
1 egg, beaten lightly
1¼ cups (310ml) milk
¼ cup (60ml) vegetable oil
caramel sauce
1 cup (220g) firmly packed brown sugar
1 cup (250ml) cream
40g butter

1 Preheat oven to 200°C/180°C fan-forced. Grease 12-hole
(⅓-cup/80ml) muffin pan.
2 Combine dates and water in small saucepan, bring to the boil.
Remove from heat, add soda, stand 5 minutes.
3 Meanwhile, sift dry ingredients into large bowl; stir in date mixture
and remaining ingredients. Do not over-mix; mixture should be lumpy.
Spoon mixture into pan holes.
4 Bake muffins about 20 minutes. Stand in pan 5 minutes before
turning onto wire rack.
5 Meanwhile, make caramel sauce.
6 Serve warm muffins drizzled with caramel sauce.
caramel sauce Stir ingredients in medium saucepan over heat, without
boiling, until sugar is dissolved. Simmer, without stirring, about 3 minutes
or until thickened slightly.

preparation time 20 minutes
cooking time 25 minutes **makes** 12
tip Fresh cream or a dollop of ice-cream makes this a delicious dessert.

Marmalade almond muffins

2 cups (300g) self-raising flour
125g butter, chopped
1 cup (80g) flaked almonds
⅔ cup (150g) caster sugar
1 tablespoon finely grated orange rind
½ cup (170g) orange marmalade
2 eggs, beaten lightly
½ cup (125ml) milk
¼ cup (20g) flaked almonds, extra
orange syrup
¼ cup (85g) orange marmalade
2 tablespoons water

1 Preheat oven to 200°C/180°C fan-forced. Grease 12-hole
(⅓-cup/80ml) muffin pan.
2 Sift flour into large bowl, rub in butter. Stir in nuts, sugar and rind,
then marmalade, egg and milk. Do not over-mix; mixture should be
lumpy. Spoon mixture into pan holes; sprinkle with extra nuts.
3 Bake muffins about 20 minutes. Stand in pan 5 minutes before
turning onto wire rack.
4 Meanwhile make orange syrup.
5 Drizzle orange syrup over warm muffins.
orange syrup Combine orange syrup ingredients in small bowl.

preparation time 15 minutes
cooking time 20 minutes **makes** 12

Citrus poppy seed muffins

125g softened butter, chopped
2 teaspoons finely grated lemon rind
2 teaspoons finely grated lime rind
2 teaspoons finely grated orange rind
⅔ cup (150g) caster sugar
2 eggs, beaten lightly
2 cups (300g) self-raising flour
½ cup (125ml) milk
2 tablespoons poppy seeds
1 medium orange (240g)
icing sugar, for dusting

1 Preheat oven to 200°C/180°C fan-forced. Grease 12-hole
(⅓-cup/80ml) muffin pan.
2 Beat butter, rinds, caster sugar, egg, sifted flour and milk in
medium bowl with electric mixer on low speed until just combined.
Increase speed to medium; beat until mixture is just changed in colour.
Stir in poppy seeds. Spoon mixture into pan holes.
3 Bake muffins about 20 minutes. Stand in pan 5 minutes before
turning onto wire rack.
4 Meanwhile, peel rind thinly from orange, avoiding any white pith.
Cut rind into thin strips. To serve, dust muffins with icing sugar;
top with orange strips.

preparation time 20 minutes
cooking time 20 minutes **makes** 12

Lime syrup coconut muffins

2½ cups (375g) self-raising flour
1 cup (90g) desiccated coconut
1 cup (220g) caster sugar
1 tablespoon finely grated lime rind
1 cup (250ml) buttermilk
125g butter, melted
2 eggs
lime syrup
½ cup (110g) caster sugar
¼ cup (60ml) water
2 teaspoons finely grated lime rind
⅓ cup (80ml) lime juice

1 Preheat oven to 200°C/180°C fan-forced. Grease 12-hole
(⅓-cup/80ml) muffin pan.
2 Combine flour, coconut and sugar in large bowl; stir in combined
remaining ingredients. Do not over-mix; mixture should be lumpy.
Spoon mixture into pan holes.
3 Bake muffins about 20 minutes.
4 Meanwhile, make lime syrup.
5 Transfer muffins to wire rack over tray; pour hot lime syrup over hot
muffins. Drain syrup from tray and pour over muffins again.
lime syrup Stir ingredients in small saucepan over heat, without boiling,
until sugar dissolves. Simmer, uncovered, without stirring, 2 minutes.

preparation time 30 minutes
cooking time 20 minutes **makes** 12

Apple and custard muffins

90g butter, melted
2 cups (300g) self-raising flour
1 cup (150g) plain flour
½ teaspoon ground cinnamon
¾ cup (165g) caster sugar
1 egg, beaten lightly
1 cup (250ml) milk
¼ cup (60ml) packaged thick custard
½ cup (110g) canned pie apples
2 tablespoons brown sugar
½ teaspoon ground cinnamon, extra

1 Preheat oven to 200°C/180°C fan-forced. Grease 12-hole
(⅓-cup/80ml) muffin pan or line with paper cases.
2 Combine butter, flours, cinnamon, caster sugar, egg and milk
in large bowl until just combined. Do not over-mix; mixture should
be lumpy.
3 Spoon half the mixture into pan holes; make well in centre of each
muffin, drop 1 level teaspoon of custard and 2 level teaspoons of
apple into each well. Top with remaining muffin mixture; sprinkle with
combined brown sugar and extra cinnamon.
4 Bake muffins about 25 minutes. Stand in pan 5 minutes before
turning onto wire rack.

preparation time 20 minutes
cooking time 25 minutes **makes** 12

Honey sultana and pecan muffins

You will need about 2 small overripe bananas (260g) for this recipe.

2 cups (300g) self-raising flour
2 teaspoons ground cinnamon
¾ cup (150g) firmly packed brown sugar
½ cup (50g) chopped pecans
½ cup (80g) sultanas
¼ cup (90g) honey
¾ cup mashed banana
¼ cup (70g) low-fat yogurt
¾ cup (180ml) low-fat milk
2 eggs, beaten lightly

1 Preheat oven to 200°C/180°C fan-forced. Grease 12-hole
(⅓-cup/80ml) muffin pan.
2 Sift flour and cinnamon into large bowl. Add sugar, nuts and sultanas,
then combined remaining ingredients; stir until just combined. Do not
over-mix; mixture should be lumpy. Spoon mixture into pan holes.
3 Bake muffins about 25 minutes. Stand in pan 5 minutes before
turning onto wire rack. Dust with sifted icing sugar and top with a
light sprinkling of cinnamon, if you like.

preparation time 15 minutes
cooking time 25 minutes **makes** 12

Overnight date and muesli muffins

1 ¼ cups (185g) plain flour
1 ¼ cups (160g) toasted muesli
1 teaspoon ground cinnamon
1 teaspoon bicarbonate of soda
½ cup (110g) firmly packed brown sugar
½ cup (30g) unprocessed bran
¾ cup (120g) coarsely chopped seeded dried dates
1 ½ cups (375ml) buttermilk
½ cup (125ml) vegetable oil
1 egg, beaten lightly

1 Stir ingredients in large bowl until just combined. Do not over-mix; mixture should be lumpy. Cover; refrigerate overnight.
2 Preheat oven to 200°C/180°C fan-forced. Grease 12-hole (⅓-cup/80ml) muffin pan.
3 Spoon muffin mixture into pan holes.
4 Bake muffins about 20 minutes. Stand in pan 5 minutes before turning onto wire rack.

preparation time 10 minutes (plus refrigeration time)
cooking time 20 minutes **makes** 12

Raspberry and coconut muffins

2½ cups (375g) self-raising flour
90g butter, chopped
1 cup (220g) caster sugar
1¼ cups (310ml) buttermilk
1 egg, beaten lightly
⅓ cup (30g) desiccated coconut
150g fresh or frozen raspberries
2 tablespoons shredded coconut

1 Preheat oven to 200°C/180°C fan-forced. Grease 12-hole
(⅓-cup/80ml) muffin pan.
2 Sift flour into large bowl; rub in butter with fingertips. Add sugar,
buttermilk, egg, desiccated coconut and raspberries; stir until just
combined. Do not over-mix; mixture should be lumpy.
3 Spoon mixture into pan holes; sprinkle with shredded coconut.
4 Bake muffins about 20 minutes. Stand in pan 5 minutes before
turning onto wire rack.

preparation time 10 minutes
cooking time 20 minutes **makes** 12
tip Two kinds of coconut – finely grated in the mix and shredded on top
– create a moist morsel with a contrasting crunch.

Gluten-free, dairy-free raspberry muffins

2½ cups (375g) gluten-free plain flour
1 tablespoon gluten-free baking powder
½ teaspoon bicarbonate of soda
⅓ cup (40g) rice bran
⅔ cup (150g) firmly packed brown sugar
1½ cups (375ml) soy milk
1 teaspoon vanilla extract
60g dairy-free spread, melted
2 eggs, beaten lightly
150g frozen raspberries
1 tablespoon coffee crystals

1 Preheat oven to 200°C/180°C fan-forced. Grease 12-hole (⅓-cup/80ml) muffin pan or line with paper cases.
2 Sift flour, baking powder and soda into large bowl. Stir in bran, sugar, combined milk, extract, spread and egg until almost combined. Add raspberries, stir until just combined.
3 Spoon mixture into pan holes; sprinkle with coffee crystals.
4 Bake muffins about 20 minutes. Stand in pan 5 minutes before turning onto wire rack.

preparation time 15 minutes
cooking time 20 minutes **makes** 12

White chocolate and macadamia muffins

2 cups (300g) self-raising flour
⅔ cup (150g) caster sugar
¾ cup (140g) white Choc Bits
½ cup (75g) coarsely chopped macadamias, roasted
60g butter, melted
¾ cup (180ml) milk
1 egg, beaten lightly

1 Preheat oven to 200°C/180°C fan-forced. Grease 6-hole texas (¾-cup/180ml) muffin pan.
2 Sift flour and sugar into large bowl; stir in remaining ingredients until just combined. Do not over-mix; mixture should be lumpy. Spoon mixture into pan holes.
3 Bake muffins about 20 minutes. Stand in pan 5 minutes before turning onto wire rack.

preparation time 10 minutes
cooking time 20 minutes **makes** 6

friands

Almond friands

6 egg whites
185g butter, melted
1 cup (120g) almond meal
1½ cups (240g) icing sugar
½ cup (75g) plain flour

1 Preheat oven to 200°C/180°C fan-forced. Grease 12 x ½ cup (125ml) pans; place on oven tray.
2 Place egg whites in medium bowl; beat with a fork. Stir in butter, almond meal and sifted icing sugar and flour until just combined.
3 Spoon mixture into pans.
4 Bake friands about 25 minutes. Stand in pans 5 minutes before turning, top-side up, onto wire rack. Serve dusted with extra sifted icing sugar, if you like.

variations
raspberry and white chocolate Stir 100g coarsely chopped white chocolate into egg-white mixture. Top friands with 100g fresh or frozen raspberries.
lime coconut Stir 2 teaspoons finely grated lime rind, 1 tablespoon lime juice and ¼ cup (20g) desiccated coconut into egg-white mixture; sprinkle unbaked friands with ⅓ cup (15g) flaked coconut.
passionfruit Use either almond or hazelnut meal, then drizzle the pulp of 2 medium passionfruit over unbaked friands.
berry Top unbaked friands with 100g fresh or frozen mixed berries.
citrus and poppy seed Add 2 teaspoons grated lemon or orange rind and 1 tablespoon poppy seeds to egg-white mixture.
chocolate and hazelnut Replace almond meal with hazelnut meal. Stir 100g coarsely chopped dark chocolate into egg-white mixture. Sprinkle unbaked friands with ¼ cup coarsely chopped hazelnuts.
plum Use hazelnut or almond meal. Top unbaked friands with 2 medium (200g) thinly sliced plums.

preparation time 20 minutes
cooking time 25 minutes **makes** 12
tip Friands are best made on the day of serving, but can be stored in an airtight container for 2 days, or frozen for up to 3 months.

Pear and almond friands

6 egg whites
185g butter, melted
1 cup (120g) almond meal
1½ cups (240g) icing sugar
¾ cup (110g) plain flour
1 small pear (180g), peeled, cored, chopped finely
¼ cup (20g) flaked almonds

1 Preheat oven to 200°C/180°C fan-forced. Grease 12-hole (⅓-cup/80ml) muffin pan.
2 Whisk egg whites with a fork in medium bowl until frothy. Stir in butter, almond meal, sifted icing sugar and flour, then pear until combined.
3 Spoon mixture into pan holes; sprinkle with nuts.
4 Bake friands about 20 minutes. Stand in pan 5 minutes before turning, top-side up, onto wire rack.

preparation time 15 minutes
cooking time 20 minutes **makes** 12

Coffee friands

6 egg whites
185g butter, melted
1 cup (125g) almond meal
1½ cups (240g) icing sugar
½ cup (75g) plain flour
1½ tablespoons ground coffee beans

1 Preheat oven to 200°C/180°C fan-forced. Grease 12 x ½ cup (125ml) oval friand pans; place on oven tray.
2 Place egg whites in medium bowl; beat with a fork. Stir in butter, almond meal, sifted icing sugar and flour, and coffee until combined. Spoon mixture into pans.
3 Bake friands about 20 minutes. Stand in pans 5 minutes before turning, top-side up, onto wire rack. Serve dusted with a little extra sifted icing sugar or cinnamon sugar, if you like.

preparation time 15 minutes
cooking time 25 minutes **makes** 12

Pistachio and hazelnut friands with toffee shards

6 egg whites
185g butter, melted
¾ cup (75g) hazelnut meal
¼ cup (35g) roasted shelled pistachios, chopped coarsely
1½ cups (240g) icing sugar
½ cup (75g) plain flour
2 teaspoons rosewater
⅓ cup (50g) roasted shelled pistachios, extra
toffee shards
⅔ cup (160ml) water
1⅓ cups (300g) caster sugar

1 Make toffee shards.
2 Preheat oven to 200°C/180°C fan-forced. Grease 8 x ½ cup (125ml) oval or rectangular friand pans; place on oven tray.
3 Place egg whites in medium bowl; beat with a fork. Stir in butter, hazelnut meal, nuts, sugar, flour and rosewater until just combined. Spoon mixture into pans; top with extra nuts.
4 Bake friands about 30 minutes. Stand in pans 5 minutes before turning, top-side up, onto wire rack.
5 Meanwhile, make toffee shards.
6 Serve friands warm or at room temperature with toffee shards and thick cream, if you like.

toffee shards Stir ingredients in small saucepan over heat, without boiling, until sugar dissolves; bring to the boil. Reduce heat; simmer, uncovered, without stirring, about 10 minutes or until toffee is golden brown. Remove from heat; allow bubbles to subside. Pour hot toffee onto lightly oiled oven tray; do not scrape the toffee from pan, or it might crystallise. Allow toffee to set at room temperature; break into shards with hands.

preparation time 20 minutes
cooking time 30 minutes **makes** 8

Cherry friands

6 egg whites
185g butter, melted
1 cup (125g) almond meal
1½ cups (240g) icing sugar
½ cup (75g) plain flour
250g fresh cherries, halved, pitted

1 Preheat oven to 200°C/180°C fan-forced. Grease 12 x ½ cup (125ml) rectangular or oval friand pans or 12-hole (⅓-cup/80ml) muffin pan; stand pans on oven tray.
2 Place egg whites in medium bowl; beat with a fork. Stir in butter, almond meal and sifted icing sugar and flour until just combined. Spoon mixture into pans; top with cherries.
3 Bake friands about 25 minutes. Stand in pans 5 minutes before turning, top-side up, onto wire rack.

preparation time 15 minutes
cooking time 25 minutes **makes** 12
tips Cherries can be frozen for up to 18 months. Freeze them, in 250g batches, when they are in season. If you use frozen cherries, be sure to use them unthawed – this will minimise the "bleeding" of colour into the mixture.

Mini choc chip friands

4 egg whites
125g butter, melted
⅔ cup (80g) almond meal
¾ cup (120g) icing sugar
¼ cup (35g) plain flour
100g dark eating chocolate, chopped finely
¼ cup (60ml) cream
100g dark eating chocolate, chopped, extra

1 Preheat oven to 200°C/180°C fan-forced. Grease two 12-hole mini
(2-tablespoons/40ml) muffin pans.
2 Place egg whites in a medium bowl; beat with a fork. Stir in butter,
almond meal, sifted icing sugar and flour and chopped chocolate.
Spoon mixture into pan holes.
3 Bake friands about 15 minutes. Stand in pans 5 minutes before
turning, top-side up, onto wire rack to cool.
4 Meanwhile, combine cream and extra chocolate in small heatproof
bowl over small saucepan of simmering water; stir until smooth.
Stand until thick. Spoon chocolate mixture over friands.

preparation time 20 minutes
cooking time 20 minutes **makes** 24

Lemon and coconut friands

6 egg whites
185g butter, melted
1 cup (100g) hazelnut meal
1½ cups (240g) icing sugar
½ cup (75g) plain flour
2 teaspoons finely grated lemon rind
1 tablespoon lemon juice
¼ cup (20g) desiccated coconut
⅓ cup (15g) flaked coconut

1 Preheat oven to 200°C/180°C fan-forced. Grease 12-hole (⅓-cup/
80ml) muffin pan.
2 Place egg whites in medium bowl; beat with fork. Stir in butter,
hazelnut meal, sifted icing sugar and flour, rind, juice and desiccated
coconut until just combined.
3 Spoon mixture into pan holes; sprinkle with flaked coconut.
4 Bake friands about 20 minutes. Stand in pan 5 minutes before turning,
top-side up, onto wire rack.

preparation time 15 minutes
cooking time 20 minutes **makes** 12

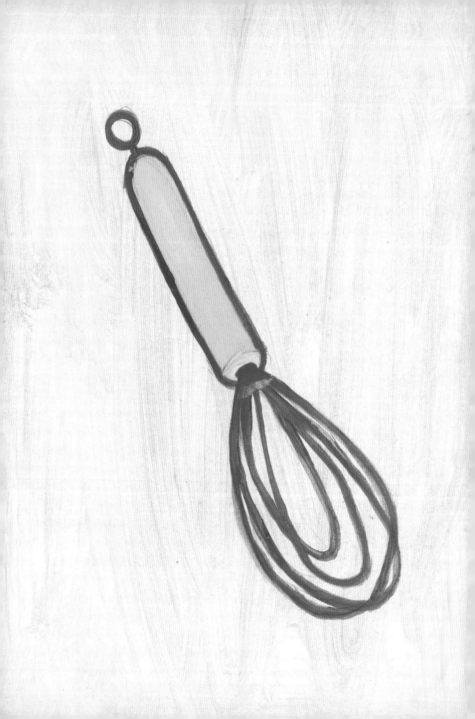

cakes

Caramel mud cake

180g white eating chocolate, chopped
185g butter, chopped
1 cup (220g) firmly packed brown sugar
⅓ cup (80ml) golden syrup
1 cup (250ml) milk
1½ cups (225g) plain flour
½ cup (75g) self-raising flour
2 eggs
white chocolate ganache
½ cup (125ml) cream
360g white eating chocolate, chopped

1 Preheat oven to 160°C/140°C fan-forced. Grease deep 22cm-round cake pan; line base with baking paper.
2 Stir chocolate, butter, sugar, syrup and milk in large saucepan over low heat until smooth. Cool 15 minutes. Whisk sifted flours and eggs into chocolate mixture. Pour mixture into pan.
3 Bake cake about 1½ hours. Cool cake in pan.
4 Meanwhile, make white chocolate ganache.
5 Turn cake, top-side up, onto plate; spread with ganache.
white chocolate ganache Bring cream to the boil in small saucepan, remove from heat; add chocolate, stir until smooth. Refrigerate, stirring occasionally, about 30 minutes or until spreadable.

preparation time 20 minutes (plus cooling and refrigeration time)
cooking time 1 hour 40 minutes **serves** 12
tip This cake can be stored in an airtight container in the refrigerator for 1 week or frozen for 2 months.

Dark chocolate mud cake

250g butter, chopped
2 cups (440g) caster sugar
½ cup (125ml) milk
½ cup (125ml) strong black coffee
½ cup (125ml) bourbon
1 teaspoon vanilla extract
200g dark eating chocolate, chopped coarsely
1½ cups (225g) plain flour
¼ cup (35g) self-raising flour
¼ cup (25g) cocoa powder
2 eggs
chocolate ganache
½ cup (125ml) cream
200g dark eating chocolate, chopped coarsely

1 Preheat oven to 160°C/140°C fan-forced. Grease deep 23cm-square cake pan; line base with baking paper.
2 Stir butter, sugar, milk, coffee, bourbon, extract and chocolate in medium saucepan over low heat until smooth. Transfer to large bowl; cool 15 minutes. Whisk in sifted flours and cocoa then eggs. Pour mixture into pan.
3 Bake cake about 1½ hours. Stand cake in pan 5 minutes; turn, top-side up, onto wire rack to cool.
4 Meanwhile, make ganache.
5 Spread cold cake with ganache.
chocolate ganache Bring cream to the boil in small saucepan. Remove from heat, add chocolate; stir until smooth. Stand 10 minutes before using.

preparation time 25 minutes (plus cooling time)
cooking time 1 hour 40 minutes **serves** 12

Dark chocolate and almond torte

160g dark eating chocolate, chopped coarsely
160g butter, chopped
5 eggs, separated
¾ cup (165g) caster sugar
1 cup (120g) almond meal
⅔ cup (50g) roasted flaked almonds, chopped coarsely
⅓ cup (35g) coarsely grated dark eating chocolate
1 cup (150g) vienna almonds
dark chocolate ganache
125g dark eating chocolate, chopped coarsely
⅓ cup (80ml) thickened cream

1 Preheat oven to 180°C/160°C fan-forced. Grease deep 22cm-round cake pan; line base and side with baking paper.
2 Stir chopped chocolate and butter in small saucepan over low heat until smooth; cool to room temperature.
3 Beat egg yolks and sugar in small bowl with electric mixer until thick and creamy. Transfer to large bowl; fold in chocolate mixture, almond meal, flaked almonds and grated chocolate.
4 Beat egg whites in small bowl with electric mixer until soft peaks form; fold into chocolate mixture, in two batches. Pour mixture into pan.
5 Bake cake about 45 minutes. Stand in pan 15 minutes before turning, top-side up, onto wire rack to cool.
6 Meanwhile, make dark chocolate ganache.
7 Spread ganache over cake, decorate cake with vienna almonds; stand 30 minutes before serving.
dark chocolate ganache Stir chocolate and cream in small saucepan over low heat until smooth.

preparation time 20 minutes
cooking time 55 minutes (plus cooling and standing time) **serves** 14
tip Vienna almonds are whole almonds coated in toffee; they are available from selected supermarkets, gourmet food and specialty confectionery stores and nut shops.

White mud cake

180g white eating chocolate, chopped
350g butter, chopped
2⅔ cups (590g) caster sugar
1½ cups (375ml) milk
2 cups (300g) plain flour
⅔ cup (100g) self-raising flour
1 teaspoon vanilla extract
3 eggs
white chocolate ganache
½ cup (125ml) cream
360g white eating chocolate, chopped

1 Preheat oven to 160°C/140°C fan-forced. Grease deep 22cm-round cake pan; line base with baking paper.
2 Stir chocolate, butter, sugar and milk in large saucepan over low heat until smooth. Pour mixture into large bowl; cool 15 minutes.
3 Whisk in sifted flours, extract and eggs. Pour mixture into pan.
4 Bake cake about 2 hours. Cool in pan.
5 Meanwhile, make white chocolate ganache.
6 Turn cake, top-side up, onto plate; spread with ganache.

white chocolate ganache Bring cream to the boil in small saucepan, remove from heat; add chocolate, stir until smooth. Refrigerate, stirring occasionally, about 30 minutes or until spreadable.

preparation time 20 minutes (plus cooling and refrigeration time)
cooking time 2 hours 10 minutes **serves** 12
tip This cake can be stored in an airtight container in the refrigerator for 1 week or frozen for 2 months.

Flourless hazelnut chocolate cake

⅓ cup (35g) cocoa powder
⅓ cup (80ml) hot water
150g dark eating chocolate, melted
150g butter, melted
1⅓ cups (275g) firmly packed brown sugar
1 cup (100g) hazelnut meal
4 eggs, separated
1 tablespoon cocoa powder, extra

1 Preheat oven to 180°C/160°C fan-forced. Grease deep 19cm-square cake pan; line base and sides with baking paper.
2 Blend cocoa with the hot water in large bowl until smooth. Stir in chocolate, butter, sugar, hazelnut meal and egg yolks.
3 Beat egg whites in small bowl with electric mixer until soft peaks form; fold into chocolate mixture in two batches. Pour mixture into pan.
4 Bake cake about 1 hour or until firm. Stand cake in pan 15 minutes; turn, top-side up, onto wire rack to cool. Dust with sifted extra cocoa.

preparation time 20 minutes (plus standing time)
cooking time 1 hour **serves** 9
tips This cake can be made up to 4 days ahead and refrigerated, covered. It can also be frozen for up to 3 months.
Hazelnut meal, also sold as ground hazelnuts, is a flour-like substance made after the nuts have been roasted

Royal Mail

Something for you

Date: 12-12 **Time:** 13:05

Name: MISS SUZANNA McGUI

Address: 16C Wembly

[handwritten] **Postcode:** _[handwritten]_

To collect:

→ If collecting you must bring this card and proof of identification (ID).

→ ID includes valid Passport, Debit/Credit Card, Driving Licence*.

→ If someone else is collecting, you must give them your ID and this card.

BRING ID

Sorry we missed you. Your item is...

☐ with your neighbour at: ☐ in your Safeplace at:

☒ Being held at your local office, ready to collect the next working day from:

North London Delivery Centre, Unit 11-13 Bush Ind Est, Station Road, LONDON N19 5UW

MON, TUE, THU, FRI: 7am – 7pm
WED: 7am – 8pm
SAT: 7am – 2pm

Or redeliver to:

→ your address (free)

→ a neighbour (free)

→ a local Post Office® branch (small fee*).

To book your redelivery, visit royalmail.com/redelivery scan the QR code or call us on 03456 021 021

*Visit royalmail.com/redelivery for a full list of ID and prices.

P739 July 14

About your item(s):

Total number of items ☐

	Letter	Parcel
Royal Mail Special Delivery Guaranteed[†]	☐	☐
Royal Mail Tracked	☐	☑
Royal Mail Signed For®	☐	☐
International – signature required[†]	☐	☐
Other	☐	☐

☐ Perishable item

We were unable to deliver because…

☑ a signature is required.

☐ it's too large for your letterbox.

Note: we keep items for 18 calendar days before returning to sender.

[†]Royal Mail Special Delivery Guaranteed and International items requiring a signature can't be redelivered to a neighbour's address.

www.royalmail.com

Please note, if ticked:

☐ This was an attempt to redeliver as you requested.

☐ The date/time on the front of this card is when we attempted delivery. We couldn't leave this card then due to restricted access.

Item reference number(s):

J	W	C	X	6	5	7	9	7	6	5

Delivery officer's initials .... Duty No ....

If you are deaf or hard-of-hearing and have access to a Textphone you can contact us on **03456 000 606.**

Chocolate cake

125g butter, softened
1 teaspoon vanilla extract
1¼ cups (275g) caster sugar
2 eggs
1⅓ cups (200g) self-raising flour
½ cup (50g) cocoa powder
⅔ cup (160ml) water
chocolate icing
90g dark eating chocolate, chopped coarsely
30g butter
1 cup (160g) icing sugar
2 tablespoons hot water

1 Preheat oven to 180°C/160°C fan-forced. Grease deep 20cm-round cake pan; line base with baking paper.
2 Beat butter, extract, sugar, eggs, sifted flour and cocoa, and the water in large bowl with electric mixer on low speed until ingredients are combined. Increase speed to medium; beat about 3 minutes or until mixture is smooth and paler in colour. Spread mixture into pan.
3 Bake cake about 1 hour. Stand cake in pan 5 minutes; turn, top-side up, onto wire rack to cool.
4 Meanwhile, make chocolate icing. Spread cake with icing.
chocolate icing Melt chocolate and butter in small heatproof bowl over small saucepan of simmering water; gradually stir in sifted icing sugar and the hot water, stirring until icing is spreadable.

preparation time 10 minutes (plus cooling time)
cooking time 1 hour **serves** 20
tip This cake can be stored in an airtight container for up to 3 days.

Boiled raisin chocolate cake

2 cups (300g) raisins
2 cups (500ml) water
1 teaspoon bicarbonate of soda
⅓ cup (35g) cocoa powder
2 teaspoons ground cinnamon
½ teaspoon ground cloves
1 teaspoon vanilla extract
250g butter, chopped
1½ cups (330g) caster sugar
4 eggs
1½ cups (225g) plain flour
1 cup (150g) self-raising flour
chocolate glaze
200g dark eating chocolate, chopped coarsely
100g butter, chopped

1 Preheat oven to 180°C/160°C fan-forced. Grease 24cm bundt pan well.
2 Combine raisins and the water in medium saucepan; bring to the boil.
Reduce heat; simmer, uncovered, 10 minutes. Remove from heat; stir in
soda, cocoa, spices and extract. Cool to room temperature.
3 Beat butter and sugar in medium bowl with electric mixer until light
and fluffy. Beat in eggs, one at a time. Stir in combined sifted flours and
raisin mixture, in two batches. Spread mixture into pan.
4 Bake cake about 1 hour 10 minutes. Stand cake in pan 5 minutes;
turn, top-side down, onto wire rack to cool.
5 Meanwhile, make chocolate glaze.
6 Pour glaze over cooled cake; stand 30 minutes before serving.
chocolate glaze Stir chocolate and butter in medium in medium
heatproof bowl over medium saucepan of simmering water until smooth.

preparation time 20 minutes
cooking time 1 hour 20 minutes (plus cooling and standing time)
serves 8
tips Raisins and other dried fruits are generally "plumped" to rehydrate
them before being stirred into a cake mixture and baked, otherwise, the
fruit is likely to remain as it is, dry, chewy and tough, rather than melt-in-
your-mouth luscious. Any raisins that have clumped will also separate
in the boiling water. Dried cranberries can be rehydrated exactly as the
raisins, and can be used instead, in this recipe.

Polenta and almond orange cake

2 medium oranges (480g)
⅔ cup (110g) roasted blanched almonds
¾ cup (165g) caster sugar
1 teaspoon baking powder
6 eggs
1 cup (120g) almond meal
1 cup (170g) polenta
50g butter, melted

1 Cover unpeeled whole oranges in medium saucepan with cold water, bring to the boil. Boil, uncovered, 30 minutes; drain. Repeat process with fresh water, boil about 1 hour or until oranges are tender; drain. Cool oranges.
2 Preheat oven to 200°C/180°C fan-forced. Grease deep 22cm-round cake pan; line base and side with baking paper.
3 Blend or process nuts with 1 tablespoon of the sugar until coarse.
4 Trim ends from oranges then cut in half; discard seeds. Blend or process oranges, including rind, with baking powder until mixture is pulpy.
5 Beat eggs with remaining sugar in small bowl with electric mixer until light and fluffy. Transfer to large bowl; fold in nut mixture, almond meal, polenta, butter and orange pulp. Spread mixture into pan.
6 Bake cake about 50 minutes. Stand cake in pan 5 minutes; turn, top-side up, onto plate. Serve dusted with sifted icing sugar, if you like.

preparation time 30 minutes (plus cooling time)
cooking time 2 hours 45 minutes **serves** 12

Chocolate banana cake

You need approximately 2 large overripe bananas (460g) for this recipe.

⅔ cup (160ml) milk
2 teaspoons lemon juice
150g butter, softened
1 cup (220g) caster sugar
2 eggs
2 cups (300g) self-raising flour
½ teaspoon bicarbonate of soda
1 cup mashed banana
100g dark eating chocolate, grated finely
creamy choc frosting
200g dark eating chocolate
1 cup (160g) icing sugar
½ cup (120g) sour cream

1 Preheat oven to 170°C/150°C fan-forced. Grease deep 22cm-round cake pan; line base with baking paper.
2 Combine milk and juice in small jug; stand 10 minutes.
3 Meanwhile, beat butter and sugar in small bowl with electric mixer until light and fluffy. Beat in eggs, one at a time, until just combined; transfer mixture to large bowl. Stir in sifted flour and soda, banana, milk mixture and chocolate. Spread mixture into pan.
4 Bake cake about 1 hour 10 minutes. Stand cake in pan 5 minutes; turn, top-side up, onto wire rack to cool.
5 Meanwhile, make creamy choc frosting.
6 Spread cold cake with frosting.
creamy choc frosting Melt chocolate in medium heatproof bowl over medium saucepan of simmering water; gradually stir in icing sugar and sour cream.

preparation time 25 minutes
cooking time 1 hour 15 minutes **serves** 8

Orange cake

150g butter, softened
1 tablespoon finely grated orange rind
⅔ cup (150g) caster sugar
3 eggs
1½ cups (225g) self-raising flour
¼ cup (60ml) milk
¾ cup (120g) icing sugar
1½ tablespoons orange juice

1 Preheat oven to 180°C/160°C fan-forced. Grease deep 20cm-round cake pan.
2 Beat butter, rind, caster sugar, eggs, flour and milk in medium bowl with electric mixer at low speed until just combined. Increase speed to medium, beat about 3 minutes or until smooth. Spread mixture into pan.
3 Bake cake about 40 minutes. Stand cake in pan 5 minutes; turn, top-side up, onto wire rack to cool.
4 Combine sifted icing sugar and juice in small bowl; spread over cake.

preparation time 10 minutes
cooking time 40 minutes **serves** 12
tip This cake can be stored in an airtight container for up to 4 days.

Ginger cake with golden ginger cream

250g butter
½ cup (110g) firmly packed brown sugar
⅔ cup (230g) golden syrup
12cm piece fresh ginger (60g), grated
1 cup (150g) plain flour
1 cup (150g) self-raising flour
½ teaspoon bicarbonate of soda
2 eggs, beaten lightly
¾ cup (180ml) thickened cream
golden ginger cream
300ml thickened cream
2 tablespoons golden syrup
2 teaspoons ground ginger

1 Preheat oven to 180°C/160°C fan-forced. Grease deep 22cm-round cake pan.
2 Melt butter in medium saucepan; add sugar, syrup and ginger. Stir over low heat until sugar dissolves. Whisk in combined sifted flours and soda then egg and cream. Pour mixture into pan.
3 Bake cake about 50 minutes. Stand cake in pan 10 minutes; turn, top-side up, onto wire rack to cool.
4 Meanwhile, make golden ginger cream. Serve cake with cream.
golden ginger cream Beat ingredients in small bowl with electric mixer until soft peaks form.

preparation time 15 minutes
cooking time 1 hour **serves** 8

Carrot and banana cake

You need approximately 4 medium carrots (480g) and 2 large overripe bananas (460g) for this recipe.

1¼ cups (185g) plain flour
½ cup (75g) self-raising flour
1 teaspoon bicarbonate of soda
1 teaspoon mixed spice
½ teaspoon ground cinnamon
1 cup (220g) firmly packed brown sugar
¾ cup (80g) coarsely chopped walnuts
3 eggs, beaten lightly
2 cups coarsely grated carrot
1 cup mashed banana
1 cup (250ml) vegetable oil
cream cheese frosting
90g packaged cream cheese
90g butter
1 cup (160g) icing sugar

1 Preheat oven to 170°C/150°C fan-forced. Grease base and side of 24cm-round springform tin; line base with baking paper.
2 Sift flours, soda, spices and sugar into large bowl. Stir in walnuts, egg, carrot, banana and oil; pour mixture into tin.
3 Bake cake about 1¼ hours. Cool cake in tin.
4 Meanwhile, make cream cheese frosting.
5 Turn cold cake onto serving plate; top with frosting.
cream cheese frosting Beat cream cheese and butter in small bowl with electric mixer until as white as possible; gradually beat in icing sugar.

preparation time 20 minutes
cooking time 1 hour 15 minutes (plus cooling time) **serves** 10
tips Pecans can be substituted for walnuts, if you like.

Date and walnut rolls

60g butter
1 cup (250ml) boiling water
1 cup (180g) finely chopped seeded dried dates
½ teaspoon bicarbonate of soda
1 cup (220g) firmly packed brown sugar
2 cups (300g) self-raising flour
½ cup (60g) coarsely chopped walnuts
1 egg, beaten lightly

1 Preheat oven to 180°C/160°C fan-forced. Grease two 8cm x 19cm nut roll tins; line bases with baking paper. Place tins upright on oven tray.
2 Stir butter and the water in medium saucepan over low heat until butter melts. Remove from heat; stir in dates and soda, then remaining ingredients. Spoon mixture into tins; replace lids.
3 Bake rolls about 50 minutes. Stand rolls in tins 5 minutes; remove ends (top and bottom), shake tins gently to release rolls onto wire rack to cool.

preparation time 15 minutes
cooking time 50 minutes (plus cooling time) **serves** 20
tips Nut roll tins are available from cookware shops and department stores. There are different sizes and types of nut roll tins available, and it is important that you do not fill them with too much mixture. As a loose guide, the tins should be filled just a little over halfway. Some nut roll tins open along the side; be certain these are closed properly before baking. Some lids have tiny holes in them to allow steam to escape; make sure these are not used on the bottom of the tins. Well-cleaned fruit juice cans may be used instead of the nut roll tins; use a double thickness of foil as a substitute for the lids.
Store fruit rolls in an airtight container for up to 3 days or freeze for up to 3 months.

Madeira cake

180g butter, softened
2 teaspoons finely grated lemon rind
⅔ cup (150g) caster sugar
3 eggs
¾ cup (110g) plain flour
¾ cup (110g) self-raising flour
⅓ cup (55g) mixed peel
¼ cup (35g) slivered almonds

1 Preheat oven to 160°C/140°C fan-forced. Grease deep 20cm-round cake pan; line base with baking paper.
2 Beat butter, rind and sugar in small bowl with electric mixer until light and fluffy. Beat in eggs, one at a time. Transfer mixture to large bowl; stir in sifted flours. Spread mixture into pan.
3 Bake cake 20 minutes. Remove from oven; sprinkle with peel and nuts. Bake further 40 minutes. Stand cake in pan 5 minutes; turn, top-side up, onto wire rack to cool.

preparation time 15 minutes
cooking time 1 hour **serves** 12
tip This cake can be stored in an airtight container for up to 4 days.

Marble cake

250g butter, softened
1 teaspoon vanilla extract
1¼ cups (275g) caster sugar
3 eggs
2¼ cups (335g) self-raising flour
¾ cup (180ml) milk
pink food colouring
2 tablespoons cocoa powder
2 tablespoons milk, extra
butter frosting
90g butter, softened
1 cup (160g) icing sugar
1 tablespoon milk

1 Preheat oven to 180°C/160°C fan-forced. Grease deep 22cm-round cake pan; line with baking paper.
2 Beat butter, extract and sugar in medium bowl with electric mixer until light and fluffy. Beat in eggs, one at a time. Stir in sifted flour and milk, in two batches.
3 Divide mixture among three bowls; tint one mixture pink. Blend sifted cocoa with extra milk in cup; stir into second mixture. Drop alternate spoonfuls of mixtures into pan. Pull a skewer backwards and forwards through cake mixture.
4 Bake cake about 1 hour. Stand cake in pan 5 minutes; turn, top-side up, onto wire rack to cool.
5 Meanwhile, make butter frosting.
6 Top marble cake with butter frosting.
butter frosting Beat butter in small bowl with electric mixer until light and fluffy; beat in sifted icing sugar and milk, in two batches. Tint pink with colouring.

preparation time 30 minutes (plus cooling time)
cooking time 1 hour **serves** 12
tip This cake can be stored, at room temperature, in an airtight container for 2 days, or can be frozen for 2 months.

Coconut yogurt cake

125g butter, softened
1 cup (220g) caster sugar
2 eggs
½ cup (40g) desiccated coconut
1 cup (150g) self-raising flour
½ cup (75g) plain flour
200g greek-style yogurt
⅔ cup (160ml) milk
frosting
2 cups (320g) icing sugar
1⅓ cups (100g) desiccated coconut
2 egg whites, beaten lightly
pink food colouring

1 Preheat oven to 180°C/160°C fan-forced. Grease deep 23cm-square cake pan; line base with baking paper.
2 Beat butter and sugar in small bowl with electric mixer until light and fluffy. Beat in eggs, one at a time. Transfer mixture to large bowl; stir in coconut, sifted flours, yogurt and milk, in two batches. Spread mixture into pan.
3 Bake cake about 40 minutes. Stand cake in pan 5 minutes; turn, top-side up, onto wire rack to cool.
4 Meanwhile, make frosting. Drop alternate spoonfuls of white and pink frosting onto cake; marble over top of cake.
frosting Sift icing sugar into medium bowl; stir in coconut and egg white. Place half the mixture in small bowl; tint with pink colouring.

preparation time 25 minutes
cooking time 40 minutes **serves** 12
tip This cake can be stored in an airtight container for up to 1 week.

Lime and poppy seed syrup cake

¼ cup (40g) poppy seeds
½ cup (125ml) milk
250g butter, softened
1 tablespoon finely grated lime rind
1¼ cups (275g) caster sugar
4 eggs
2¼ cups (335g) self-raising flour
¾ cup (110g) plain flour
1 cup (240g) sour cream
lime syrup
½ cup (125ml) lime juice
1 cup (250ml) water
1 cup (220g) caster sugar

1 Preheat oven to 180°C/160°C fan-forced. Grease deep 23cm-square cake pan.
2 Combine poppy seeds and milk in small jug; soak 10 minutes.
3 Beat butter, rind and sugar in small bowl with electric mixer until light and fluffy. Beat in eggs, one at a time. Transfer mixture to large bowl; stir in sifted flours, sour cream and poppy seed mixture, in two batches. Spread mixture into pan.
4 Bake cake about 1 hour. Stand cake in pan 5 minutes; turn, top-side up, onto wire rack over tray.
5 Meanwhile, make lime syrup; pour hot syrup over hot cake.
lime syrup Stir ingredients in small saucepan over heat, without boiling, until sugar dissolves. Simmer, uncovered, without stirring, 5 minutes.

preparation time 20 minutes **cooking time** 1 hour **serves** 9
tips Before grating the lime, make sure it is at room temperature and roll it, pressing down hard with your hand, on the kitchen bench. This will help extract as much juice as possible from the fruit.
You can substitute the same weight of other citrus fruit – lemons, mandarins, blood oranges, oranges, etc – for the limes if you like.

Sponge roll with jam and cream

3 eggs
⅔ cup (150g) caster sugar
½ cup (75g) wheaten cornflour
2 tablespoons custard powder
¾ teaspoon cream of tartar
½ teaspoon bicarbonate of soda
⅓ cup (110g) raspberry jam
¾ cup (180ml) thickened cream, whipped

1 Preheat oven to 180°C/160°C fan-forced. Grease 25cm x 30cm swiss roll pan; line base with baking paper, extending paper 5cm over long sides.
2 Beat eggs and ½ cup of the caster sugar in small bowl with electric mixer until thick, creamy and sugar has dissolved. Fold in triple-sifted dry ingredients. Spread mixture into pan.
3 Bake cake about 12 minutes.
4 Meanwhile, place piece of baking paper cut the same size as pan on bench; sprinkle with remaining caster sugar. Turn sponge onto paper; peel lining paper away. Cool; trim all sides of sponge.
5 Spread sponge with jam then cream. Using paper as a guide, roll sponge from short side. Cover with plastic wrap; refrigerate 30 minutes.

preparation time 25 minutes (plus refrigeration time)
cooking time 12 minutes **serves** 10
tip Filled sponges and rolls are best eaten on the day they are made.

Mixed berry cake with vanilla bean syrup

125g butter, chopped
1 cup (220g) caster sugar
3 eggs
½ cup (75g) plain flour
¼ cup (35g) self-raising flour
½ cup (60g) almond meal
⅓ cup (80g) sour cream
1½ cups (225g) frozen mixed berries
½ cup (100g) drained canned seeded black cherries
vanilla bean syrup
½ cup (125ml) water
½ cup (110g) caster sugar
2 vanilla beans

1 Preheat oven to 180°C/160°C fan-forced. Grease 20cm baba pan thoroughly.
2 Beat butter and sugar in small bowl with electric mixer until light and fluffy. Beat in eggs, one at a time. (Mixture will curdle at this stage, but will come together later.) Transfer mixture to large bowl; stir in sifted flours, almond meal, sour cream, berries and cherries. Pour mixture into pan.
3 Bake cake about 40 minutes.
4 Meanwhile, make vanilla bean syrup.
5 Stand cake in pan 5 minutes; turn onto wire rack placed over large tray. Pour hot syrup over hot cake.

vanilla bean syrup Combine the water and sugar in small saucepan. Split vanilla beans in half lengthways; scrape seeds into pan then add pods. Stir over heat, without boiling, until sugar dissolves. Simmer, uncovered, without stirring, 5 minutes. Using tongs, remove pods from syrup.

preparation time 20 minutes
cooking time 40 minutes **serves** 8

Vanilla pear almond cake

8 corella pears (800g)
2½ cups (625ml) water
1 strip lemon rind
1¾ cups (385g) caster sugar
1 vanilla bean
125g butter, chopped
3 eggs
⅔ cup (160g) sour cream
⅔ cup (100g) plain flour
⅔ cup (100g) self-raising flour
¼ cup (40g) blanched almonds, roasted, chopped coarsely
40g dark eating chocolate, chopped coarsely
½ cup (60g) almond meal

1 Peel pears, leaving stems intact.
2 Combine the water, rind and 1 cup of the sugar in medium saucepan.
Split vanilla bean in half lengthways; scrape seeds into saucepan,
then place pod in saucepan. Stir over heat, without boiling, until sugar
dissolves. Add pears; bring to the boil. Reduce heat; simmer, covered,
about 30 minutes or until pears are just tender. Transfer pears to medium
bowl; bring syrup to the boil. Boil, uncovered, until syrup reduces by half.
Cool completely.
3 Preheat oven to 160°C/140°C fan-forced. Insert base of 23cm
springform tin upside down in tin to give a flat base; grease tin.
4 Beat butter and remaining sugar in medium bowl with electric mixer
until light and fluffy. Beat in eggs, one at a time. Add sour cream; beat
until just combined (mixture may curdle at this stage but will come
together later). Stir in 2 tablespoons of the syrup, then flours, nuts,
chocolate and almond meal.
5 Spread cake mixture into tin; place pears upright around edge of tin,
gently pushing to the bottom.
6 Bake cake about 1 hour 35 minutes. Stand in pan10 minutes; remove
from tin. Serve warm, brushed with remaining syrup.

preparation time 30 minutes (plus cooling time)
cooking time 2 hours 15 minutes **serves** 8
tip Corella pears are miniature dessert pears with pale flesh and a sweet,
mild flavour.

Vanilla butter cake

125g butter, chopped
¾ cup (180ml) milk
3 eggs
1 tablespoon vanilla extract
1 cup (220g) caster sugar
1½ cups (225g) self-raising flour

1 Preheat oven to 180°C/160°C fan-forced. Grease deep 19cm-square cake pan; line base with baking paper.
2 Stir butter and milk in small saucepan over heat until butter is melted. Remove from heat; cool to room temperature.
3 Beat eggs and extract in small bowl with electric mixer until thick and creamy; gradually add sugar, beat until dissolved between each addition. Transfer mixture to large bowl; stir in sifted flour and butter mixture, in two batches. Pour mixture into pan.
4 Bake cake about 45 minutes. Stand cake in pan 5 minutes; turn, top-side up, onto wire rack to cool. Dust cold cake with sifted icing sugar, if you like.

preparation time 30 minutes
cooking time 50 minutes (plus cooling time) **serves** 9
tip This cake can be stored in an airtight container for up to 3 days.

Pistachio buttercake
with orange honey syrup

2 cups (280g) unsalted pistachios, chopped coarsely
185g butter, softened
1 tablespoon finely grated orange rind
¾ cup (165g) caster sugar
3 eggs
¼ cup (60ml) buttermilk
1½ cups (225g) self-raising flour
¾ cup (110g) plain flour
orange honey syrup
1 cup (220g) caster sugar
1 cup (250ml) water
1 tablespoon honey
1 cinnamon stick
1 teaspoon cardamom seeds
3 star anise
3 strips orange rind

1 Make orange honey syrup; cool.
2 Preheat oven to 180°C/160°C fan-forced. Grease 23cm-square slab
cake pan; line base and sides with baking paper, extending paper 2cm
over the sides. Sprinkle nuts evenly over base of pan.
3 Beat butter, rind and sugar in small bowl with electric mixer until light
and fluffy. Beat in eggs, one at a time. Transfer mixture to large bowl.
Stir in combined buttermilk and ⅓ cup of the orange honey syrup, and
sifted flours, in two batches. Spread mixture into pan.
4 Bake cake about 40 minutes. Stand cake in pan 5 minutes; turn,
top-side up, onto baking-paper-covered wire rack.
5 Brush surface of hot cake with half of the remaining heated syrup.
Cut cake into squares; serve warm, drizzled with remaining heated syrup.
orange honey syrup Stir ingredients in small saucepan over low heat,
without boiling, until sugar dissolves; bring to the boil. Remove from heat;
cool 15 minutes then strain.

preparation time 20 minutes
cooking time 50 minutes **serves** 9

Passionfruit and lemon syrup cake

You need approximately 7 passionfruit for this recipe.

⅔ cup (160ml) passionfruit pulp
250g butter, softened
1 tablespoon finely grated lemon rind
1 cup (220g) caster sugar
3 eggs
1 cup (250ml) buttermilk
2 cups (300g) self-raising flour
lemon syrup
⅓ cup (80ml) lemon juice
¼ cup (60ml) water
¾ cup (165g) caster sugar

1 Preheat oven to 180°C/160°C fan-forced. Grease deep 19cm-square cake pan well; line base and sides with baking paper.
2 Strain passionfruit over medium jug; reserve both juice and seeds.
3 Beat butter, rind and sugar in small bowl with electric mixer until light and fluffy. Beat in eggs, one at a time. Transfer mixture to large bowl. Fold in combined passionfruit juice and buttermilk, and sifted flour, in two batches. Spread mixture into pan.
4 Bake cake about 1 hour.
5 Meanwhile, make lemon syrup.
6 Stand cake in pan 5 minutes; turn, top-side up, onto wire rack set over tray. Pour hot syrup over hot cake; serve warm.
lemon syrup Stir juice, the water, sugar and half of the reserved passionfruit seeds (discard remaining seeds or freeze for future use) in small saucepan over heat, without boiling, until sugar dissolves. Simmer, uncovered, without stirring, 5 minutes.

preparation time 20 minutes
cooking time 1 hour **serves** 9

Genoise sponge

This is a light-textured sponge; the mixture is beaten over hot water
to give volume and extra lightness. It is correct that plain flour is used.
Melted butter should be cooled to room temperature before being added.

4 eggs
½ cup (110g) caster sugar
⅔ cup (100g) plain flour
60g butter, melted
300ml thickened cream
1 tablespoon icing sugar
¼ cup (80g) strawberry jam, warmed
500g strawberries, sliced thinly
1 tablespoon icing sugar, extra

1 Preheat oven to 180°C/160°C fan-forced. Grease deep 20cm-round
cake pan; line base with baking paper.
2 Place eggs and caster sugar in large heatproof bowl over large
saucepan simmering water. Do not allow water to touch base of bowl.
Beat with electric mixer until thick and creamy, about 10 minutes.
Remove bowl from pan; beat mixture until it returns to room temperature.
3 Sift half of the triple-sifted flour over egg mixture, carefully fold in flour;
fold in remaining sifted flour. Quickly and carefully fold in cooled butter.
Pour mixture into pan.
4 Bake sponge about 20 minutes. Turn, top-side up, onto baking-paper-
covered wire rack to cool.
5 Beat cream and sifted icing sugar in small bowl with electric mixer
until soft peaks form. Split sponge in half; place one half, cut-side up,
on serving plate. Spread with jam and cream; top with strawberries,
then remaining sponge half. Dust with extra sifted icing sugar and
strawberries, if you like.

preparation time 20 minutes (plus standing time)
cooking time 35 minutes (plus cooling time) **serves** 8
tip Unfilled cake can be frozen for up to 1 month.

Brown sugar sponge

4 eggs
¾ cup (165g) firmly packed dark brown sugar
1 cup (150g) wheaten cornflour
1 teaspoon cream of tartar
½ teaspoon bicarbonate of soda
300ml thickened cream
praline
⅓ cup (75g) sugar
¼ cup (60ml) water
½ teaspoon malt vinegar
⅓ cup (45g) roasted hazelnuts

1 Preheat oven to 180°C/160°C fan-forced. Grease two deep 22cm-round cake pans.
2 Beat eggs and sugar in small bowl with electric mixer until thick and creamy and sugar is dissolved. Transfer mixture to large bowl; fold in triple-sifted dry ingredients. Divide mixture between pans.
3 Bake cakes about 18 minutes. Turn cakes, top-side up, onto baking-paper-covered wire racks to cool.
4 Meanwhile, make praline.
5 Beat cream in small bowl with electric mixer until firm peaks form; fold in praline. Place one sponge on serving plate; spread with half of the cream mixture. Top with remaining sponge; spread with remaining cream mixture.
praline Stir sugar, the water and vinegar in small saucepan over heat, without boiling, until sugar dissolves; bring to the boil. Reduce heat; simmer, uncovered, without stirring, about 10 minutes or until syrup is golden brown. Add nuts; pour praline mixture onto baking-paper-lined tray. Cool about 15 minutes or until set. Break praline into pieces then blend or process until mixture is as fine (or coarse) as desired.

preparation time 30 minutes
cooking time 20 minutes (plus cooling time) **serves** 10

Apple custard teacake

200g butter, softened
½ cup (110g) caster sugar
2 eggs
1¼ cups (185g) self-raising flour
⅓ cup (40g) custard powder
2 medium green apples (300g), peeled, cored, sliced thinly
1 tablespoon butter, melted
2 teaspoons caster sugar, extra
½ teaspoon ground cinnamon
custard
2 tablespoons custard powder
¼ cup (55g) caster sugar
1 cup (250ml) milk
20g butter
2 teaspoons vanilla extract

1 Make custard.
2 Preheat oven to 180°C/160°C fan-forced. Grease deep 22cm-round cake pan; line base with baking paper.
3 Beat butter and sugar in small bowl with electric mixer until light and fluffy. Beat in eggs, one at a time. Stir in sifted flour and custard powder.
4 Spread half the mixture into pan, top with custard. Top custard with spoonfuls of remaining cake mixture; gently spread with spatula to completely cover custard. Arrange apples on top; brush with melted butter then sprinkle with combined extra sugar and cinnamon.
5 Bake cake about 1¼ hours; cool in pan. Sprinkle with extra caster sugar, if you like.
custard Combine custard powder and sugar in small saucepan; gradually add milk, stirring over heat until mixture thickens slightly. Remove from heat; stir in butter and extract. Press plastic wrap over surface of custard to prevent a skin forming; cool. Just before using, whisk until smooth.

preparation time 30 minutes
cooking time 1 hour 20 minutes (plus cooling time) **serves** 8
tip This cake is best made on the day of serving; refrigerate, covered, until required. It can be frozen for up to 3 months.

Ginger fluff roll

3 eggs
⅔ cup (150g) caster sugar
⅔ cup (100g) wheaten cornflour
1 teaspoon cream of tartar
½ teaspoon bicarbonate of soda
1 teaspoon cocoa powder
2 teaspoons ground ginger
½ teaspoon ground cinnamon
¾ cup (180ml) thickened cream
2 tablespoons golden syrup
1 teaspoon ground ginger, extra

1 Preheat oven to 180°C/160°C fan-forced. Grease 25cm x 30cm swiss roll pan; line base with baking paper, extending paper 5cm over long sides.
2 Beat eggs and ½ cup of the sugar in small bowl with electric mixer until thick and creamy and sugar is dissolved. Transfer mixture to large bowl; fold in triple-sifted dry ingredients. Spread mixture into pan.
3 Bake about 12 minutes.
4 Meanwhile, place piece of baking paper cut the same size as pan on bench; sprinkle with remaining sugar. Turn sponge onto paper; peel lining paper away. Cool; trim all sides of sponge.
5 Beat cream, syrup and extra ginger in small bowl with electric mixer until firm peaks form; spread over sponge. Using paper as a guide, roll sponge from long side. Cover with plastic wrap; refrigerate 30 minutes.

preparation time 25 minutes (plus refrigeration time)
cooking time 12 minutes **serves** 10
tip Filled sponges and rolls are best eaten on the day they are made. Unfilled sponges can be frozen for up to 2 months.

Lemon cake

125g butter, softened
2 teaspoons finely grated lemon rind
1¼ cups (275g) caster sugar
3 eggs
1½ cups (225g) self-raising flour
½ cup (125ml) milk
¼ cup (60ml) lemon juice
lemon mascarpone frosting
300ml thickened cream
½ cup (80g) icing sugar
2 teaspoons finely grated lemon rind
150g mascarpone cheese

1 Preheat oven to 180°C/160°C fan-forced. Grease deep 20cm-round cake pan; line base with baking paper.
2 Meanwhile, make lemon mascarpone frosting. Cover; refrigerate until required.
3 Beat butter, rind and sugar in small bowl with electric mixer until light and fluffy. Beat in eggs, one at a time. Transfer mixture to large bowl. Stir in sifted flour, milk and juice, in two batches. Pour mixture into pan.
4 Bake cake about 50 minutes. Stand cake in pan 5 minutes; turn, top-side up, onto wire rack to cool.
5 Split cold cake into three layers, place one layer onto serving plate, cut-side up; spread with one-third of the frosting. Repeat layering process, finishing with frosting.
lemon mascarpone frosting Beat cream, sifted icing sugar and rind in small bowl with electric mixer until soft peaks form. Fold cream mixture into mascarpone.

preparation time 20 minutes
cooking time 1 hour **serves** 10
tip Grate the lemon for the frosting before you squeeze the juice for the cake mixture.

137

Banana cake with passionfruit icing

You need approximately 2 large overripe bananas (460g) and
2 large passionfruit for this recipe.

125g butter, softened
¾ cup (165g) firmly packed brown sugar
2 eggs
1½ cups (225g) self-raising flour
½ teaspoon bicarbonate of soda
1 teaspoon mixed spice
1 cup mashed banana
½ cup (120g) sour cream
¼ cup (60ml) milk
passionfruit icing
1½ cups (240g) icing sugar
2 tablespoons passionfruit pulp, approximately

1 Preheat oven to 180°C/160°C fan-forced. Grease 15cm x 25cm
loaf pan; line base with baking paper.
2 Beat butter and sugar in small bowl with electric mixer until light and
fluffy. Beat in eggs, one at a time. Transfer to large bowl; stir in sifted
dry ingredients, banana, sour cream and milk. Spread mixture into pan.
3 Bake cake about 50 minutes. Stand cake in pan 5 minutes; turn,
top-side up, onto wire rack to cool.
4 Meanwhile, make passionfruit icing. Spread cake with icing.
passionfruit icing Sift icing sugar into small bowl; stir in enough of
the passionfruit to give a thin pouring consistency.

preparation time 35 minutes
cooking time 50 minutes **serves** 10
tip This cake can be stored in an airtight container for up to 4 days.

Almond carrot cake

5 eggs, separated
1 teaspoon finely grated lemon rind
1¼ cups (275g) caster sugar
2 cups (480g) coarsely grated carrot
2 cups (240g) almond meal
½ cup (75g) self-raising flour
2 tablespoons roasted slivered almonds
cream cheese frosting
100g packaged cream cheese, softened
80g butter, softened
1 teaspoon lemon juice
½ cup (80g) icing sugar

1 Preheat oven to 180°C/160°C fan-forced. Grease deep 19cm-square cake pan; line base with baking paper.
2 Beat egg yolks, rind and sugar in small bowl with electric mixer until thick and creamy. Transfer mixture to large bowl; stir in carrot, almond meal and sifted flour.
3 Beat egg whites in small bowl with electric mixer until soft peaks form; fold into carrot mixture in two batches. Pour mixture into pan.
4 Bake cake about 1¼ hours. Stand cake in pan 5 minutes; turn, top-side up, onto wire rack to cool.
5 Meanwhile, make cream cheese frosting.
6 Spread cold cake with frosting; sprinkle with slivered almonds.
cream cheese frosting Beat cream cheese and butter in small bowl with electric mixer until light and fluffy; gradually beat in juice and sugar.

preparation time 20 minutes
cooking time 1 hour 15 minutes **serves** 12

Blueberry and olive oil cake

3 eggs
1¼ cups (275g) caster sugar
2 tablespoons finely grated orange rind
½ cup (125ml) olive oil
⅓ cup (80ml) milk
1 cup (150g) plain flour
1 cup (150g) self-raising flour
100g frozen blueberries
¼ cup (80g) apricot jam, warmed, strained

1 Preheat oven to 180°C/160°C fan-forced. Grease deep 19cm-square cake pan.
2 Beat eggs, sugar and rind in small bowl with electric mixer until sugar is dissolved. Transfer mixture to large bowl; fold in combined oil and milk, and sifted flours, in two batches. Pour mixture into pan.
3 Bake cake 20 minutes. Carefully remove from oven; sprinkle surface evenly with blueberries. Return cake to oven; bake further 40 minutes.
4 Stand cake in pan 10 minutes; turn, top-side up, onto wire rack to cool. Brush warm cake with jam; serve warm with crème fraîche, if you like.

preparation time 25 minutes
cooking time 1 hour (plus standing time) **serves** 16
tips Fresh as well as frozen blueberries can be used in this cake. Don't thaw the frozen fruit, however, because it's possible that the colour might bleed into the cake. The surface of the partially cooked cake should be flat and just set before sprinkling with blueberries, to ensure that the berries don't sink during the remaining baking time.

Tiramisu roulade

2 tablespoons coffee-flavoured liqueur
¼ cup (60ml) water
2 tablespoons caster sugar
1 tablespoon instant coffee granules
1 tablespoon boiling water
3 eggs
½ cup (110g) caster sugar, extra
½ cup (75g) plain flour
2 tablespoons flaked almonds
coffee liqueur cream
250g mascarpone cheese
½ cup (125ml) thickened cream
2 tablespoons coffee-flavoured liqueur

1 Preheat oven to 220°C/200°C fan-forced. Grease 25cm x 30cm swiss roll pan; line base and two long sides with baking paper, extending paper 5cm over sides.
2 Place liqueur, the water and sugar in small saucepan; bring to the boil. Reduce heat; simmer, uncovered, without stirring, 5 minutes or until syrup thickens slightly. Remove from heat, stir in half of the coffee; reserve syrup.
3 Dissolve remaining coffee in the boiling water.
4 Beat eggs and extra sugar in small bowl with electric mixer about 5 minutes or until thick, creamy and sugar dissolves. Transfer to large bowl; fold in dissolved coffee. Fold in triple-sifted flour. Spread mixture into pan; sprinkle with almonds. Bake about 15 minutes.
5 Meanwhile, place a piece of baking paper cut the same size as pan on bench; sprinkle evenly with about 2 teaspoons of caster sugar. Turn sponge onto paper; peel lining paper away. Trim all sides of sponge. Using paper as guide, roll sponge from long side; cool.
6 Meanwhile, make coffee liqueur cream.
7 Unroll sponge, brush with reserved syrup; spread with cream then re-roll sponge. Cover with plastic wrap; refrigerate 30 minutes before serving.
coffee liqueur cream Beat ingredients in small bowl with electric mixer until firm peaks form.

preparation time 35 minutes
cooking time 20 minutes (plus refrigeration time) **serves** 10
tip Use any coffee-flavoured liqueur you prefer in the mascarpone cream filling, or try chocolate, almond or hazelnut, licorice or mint liqueur.

Kumara and pecan loaf

200g butter, softened
¾ cup (165g) firmly packed brown sugar
2 eggs
¾ cup (90g) pecans, chopped coarsely
½ cup (40g) desiccated coconut
1 cup mashed kumara
1½ cups (225g) self-raising flour
½ cup (125ml) milk

1 Preheat oven to 170°C/150°C fan-forced. Grease 14cm x 21cm loaf pan; line base and long sides with baking paper, extending paper 2cm over sides.
2 Beat butter, sugar and eggs in small bowl with electric mixer until just combined. Transfer mixture to large bowl; fold in nuts, coconut and kumara. Stir in sifted flour and milk, in two batches. Spread mixture into pan.
3 Bake loaf about 1 hour 40 minutes. Stand loaf in pan 10 minutes; turn, top-side up, onto wire rack to cool.

preparation time 20 minutes
cooking time 1 hour 40 minutes **serves** 10

Upside-down toffee date and banana cake

You need 1 large overripe banana (230g) for the mashed banana.

1½ cups (330g) caster sugar
1½ cups (375ml) water
3 star anise
2 medium bananas (400g), sliced thinly
1 cup (140g) seeded dried dates
¾ cup (180ml) water, extra
½ cup (125ml) dark rum
1 teaspoon bicarbonate of soda
60g butter, chopped
½ cup (110g) firmly packed brown sugar
2 eggs
2 teaspoons mixed spice
1 cup (150g) self-raising flour
½ cup mashed banana
300ml thickened cream

1 Preheat oven to 180°C/160°C fan-forced. Grease deep 22cm-round cake pan; line base with baking paper.
2 Stir caster sugar, the water and star anise in medium saucepan over low heat, without boiling, until sugar dissolves. Bring to the boil; boil syrup, uncovered, without stirring, about 5 minutes or until thickened slightly. Strain ½ cup of the syrup into small heatproof jug; reserve to flavour cream. Discard star anise.
3 To make toffee, continue boiling remaining syrup, uncovered, without stirring, about 10 minutes or until golden brown. Pour hot toffee into cake pan; top with sliced banana.
4 Place dates, the extra water and rum in small saucepan; bring to the boil, remove from heat. Stir in soda; stand 5 minutes. Process date mixture with butter and brown sugar until almost smooth. Add eggs, spice and flour; process until just combined. Stir in mashed banana. Pour mixture into pan.
5 Bake cake about 40 minutes. Turn cake, in pan, onto serving plate; stand 2 minutes. Remove pan then peel away baking paper.
6 To make star anise cream, beat cream in small bowl with electric mixer until firm peaks form. Stir in reserved syrup.
7 Serve cake warm or at room temperature with star anise cream.
preparation time 20 minutes
cooking time 1 hour 10 minutes **serves** 12

Spices of the orient teacake

60g butter, softened
1 teaspoon vanilla extract
½ cup (110g) caster sugar
1 egg
1 cup (150g) self-raising flour
⅓ cup (80ml) milk
20g butter, melted, extra
spiced nuts
2 tablespoons finely chopped pistachios
2 tablespoons finely chopped blanched almonds
2 tablespoons finely chopped pine nuts
¼ cup (40g) icing sugar
½ teaspoon ground allspice
½ teaspoon ground cardamom
1 teaspoon ground cinnamon

1 Preheat oven to 180°C/160°C fan-forced. Grease 20cm-round cake pan.
2 Beat butter, extract, sugar and egg in small bowl with electric mixer until light and fluffy. Stir in sifted flour and milk. Spread mixture into pan.
3 Bake cake about 25 minutes. Stand cake in pan 5 minutes; turn, top-side up, onto wire rack to cool.
4 Meanwhile, make spiced nuts.
5 Brush cake with extra butter; sprinkle with spiced nuts. Serve warm.
spiced nuts Rinse nuts in strainer under cold water. Spread wet nuts onto oven tray, sprinkle with sifted dry ingredients. Roast in oven about 10 minutes or until dry.

preparation time 20 minutes
cooking time 25 minutes **serves** 10

Matzo honey cake

3 eggs, separated
1½ cups (180g) matzo meal
2 teaspoons finely grated orange rind
¼ teaspoon ground clove
1 teaspoon ground cinnamon
⅔ cup (160ml) orange juice
¾ cup (270g) honey
½ cup (110g) firmly packed brown sugar
1 tablespoon icing sugar

1 Preheat oven to 180°C/160°C fan-forced. Grease base of deep 22cm-round cake pan; line base with baking paper.
2 Combine egg yolks, matzo, rind, spices, juice, honey and brown sugar in large bowl.
3 Beat egg whites in small bowl with electric mixer until soft peaks form; fold into matzo mixture, in two batches. Pour cake mixture into pan.
4 Bake cake about 40 minutes. Stand cake in pan 5 minutes; turn, top-side up, onto wire rack to cool. Serve dusted with sifted icing sugar.

preparation time 15 minutes
cooking time 40 minutes **serves** 8
tip Matzo meal can be found in some supermarkets and delicatessens. If you can't find it, make your own by processing matzo crackers, biscuit-like unleavened bread, found in boxes on most supermarket shelves. It's important to use regular honey in the matzo cake, not the easy-to-pour liquefied version.

Date and maple loaf

¾ cup (110g) finely chopped dried dates
⅓ cup (80ml) boiling water
½ teaspoon bicarbonate of soda
¼ cup (90g) maple syrup
90g butter, softened
⅓ cup (75g) firmly packed brown sugar
2 eggs
¾ cup (120g) wholemeal self-raising flour
½ cup (75g) plain flour
maple butter
125g butter, softened
2 tablespoons maple syrup

1 Preheat oven to 180°C/160°C fan-forced. Grease 14cm x 21cm loaf pan.
2 Combine dates and the water in small heatproof bowl. Stir in soda; cover, stand 5 minutes. Stir in maple syrup.
3 Meanwhile, beat butter and sugar in medium bowl with electric mixer until light and fluffy. Beat in eggs, one at a time (mixture may curdle at this stage but will come together later). Add butter mixture to date mixture; stir in sifted flours, in two batches. Spread mixture into pan.
4 Bake loaf about 50 minutes. Stand loaf in pan 10 minutes; turn, top-side up, onto wire rack to cool.
5 Meanwhile, make maple butter. Serve loaf with maple butter.
maple butter Whisk ingredients together in small bowl until combined.

preparation time 20 minutes
cooking time 50 minutes **serves** 8
tip Use pure maple syrup for a wonderful flavour as the imitation maple-flavoured syrup is just that.

Yogurt fruit loaf

100g butter, softened
2 teaspoons finely grated orange rind
¾ cup (165g) caster sugar
2 eggs
2 cups (320g) wholemeal self-raising flour
1 cup (280g) yogurt
⅓ cup (80ml) orange juice
1 cup (200g) finely chopped dried figs
1 cup (150g) coarsely chopped raisins

1 Preheat oven to 180°C/160°C fan-forced. Grease 14cm x 21cm loaf pan.
2 Beat butter, rind, sugar, eggs, flour, yogurt and juice in medium bowl with electric mixer, on low speed, until just combined. Stir in fruit. Pour mixture into pan; cover with foil.
3 Bake loaf 1¼ hours. Remove foil; bake further 15 minutes. Stand loaf in pan 10 minutes; turn, top-side up, onto wire rack to cool.
4 Serve loaf slices at room temperature or toasted, with butter.

preparation time 20 minutes
cooking time 1 hour 30 minutes **serves** 10
tips Use full cream plain yogurt, not a light or low-fat variation in the mixture to ensure the quality of the finished product.
Make a long, fairly wide pleat in the foil covering the pan to allow the fruit loaf to expand during baking.

Glacé fruit cake

185g butter, softened
½ cup (110g) caster sugar
3 eggs
1 cup (250g) finely chopped glacé apricot
½ cup (80g) finely chopped glacé orange
½ cup (90g) finely chopped glacé ginger
¾ cup (210g) finely chopped glacé fig
1½ cups (225g) plain flour
½ cup (75g) self-raising flour
½ cup (125ml) milk
¼ cup (60ml) ginger wine
ginger syrup
¼ cup (60ml) ginger wine
¼ cup (60ml) water
¼ cup (55g) caster sugar
2 teaspoons lemon juice

1 Preheat oven to 150°C/130°C fan-forced. Grease 14cm x 21cm
loaf pan; line base and two long sides with baking paper, extending
paper 2cm above sides.
2 Beat butter and sugar in small bowl with electric mixer until just
combined. Beat in eggs, one at a time. Transfer mixture to large bowl;
stir in fruit then sifted flours, and combined milk and wine, in two batches.
Spread mixture into pan.
3 Bake about 2½ hours.
4 Meanwhile, make ginger syrup. Pour hot syrup over hot cake in pan.
Cover with foil; cool in pan.
ginger syrup Stir ingredients in small saucepan over low heat, without
boiling, until sugar dissolves; bring to the boil. Boil, uncovered, without
stirring, about 2 minutes or until syrup thickens slightly.

preparation time 20 minutes
cooking time 2 hours 30 minutes **serves** 10
tips You can substitute the ginger wine with dry (white) vermouth, if you
like. Any type or combination of glacé fruit can be used in this recipe.

Whipped cream cake with caramel icing

600ml thickened cream
3 eggs
1 teaspoon vanilla extract
1¼ cups (275g) firmly packed brown sugar
2 cups (300g) self-raising flour
caramel icing
60g butter
½ cup (110g) firmly packed brown sugar
2 tablespoons milk
½ cup (80g) icing sugar

1 Preheat oven to 180°C/160°C fan-forced. Grease deep 22cm-round cake pan; line base with baking paper.
2 Beat half of the cream in small bowl with electric mixer until soft peaks form.
3 Beat eggs and extract in another small bowl with electric mixer until thick and creamy; gradually add sugar, beating until dissolved between additions. Transfer mixture to large bowl; fold in a quarter of the whipped cream then sifted flour, then remaining whipped cream. Spread mixture into pan.
4 Bake cake about 50 minutes. Stand cake in pan 5 minutes; turn, top-side up, onto wire rack to cool.
5 Meanwhile, beat remaining cream in small bowl with electric mixer until firm peaks form.
6 Make caramel icing.
7 Split cold cake in half; sandwich layers with cream. Spread cake with caramel icing.
caramel icing Melt butter in small saucepan, add brown sugar and milk; bring to the boil. Reduce heat immediately; simmer 2 minutes. Cool. Stir in sifted icing sugar.

preparation time 20 minutes
cooking time 50 minutes (plus cooling time) **serves** 10
tip Cream takes the place of butter in this recipe, giving this cake a firm but fine texture.

Caramelised apple buttercake

2 medium apples (300g)
80g butter
¾ cup (165g) firmly packed brown sugar
125g butter, softened, extra
⅔ cup (150g) caster sugar
1 teaspoon vanilla extract
2 eggs
1 cup (150g) self-raising flour
⅔ cup (100g) plain flour
½ teaspoon bicarbonate of soda
1 cup (250ml) buttermilk
¾ cup (180ml) cream

1 Preheat oven to 180°C/160°C fan-forced. Grease 20cm bundt pan.
2 Peel, core and quarter apples; slice thinly. Melt butter in large frying pan; cook apple about 5 minutes or until browned lightly. Add brown sugar; cook, stirring, about 5 minutes or until mixture thickens slightly. Strain apples over medium bowl. Reserve apples and cooking liquid.
3 Beat extra butter, caster sugar and extract in small bowl with electric mixer until light and fluffy. Beat in eggs, one at a time. Transfer mixture to large bowl; stir in sifted dry ingredients and buttermilk, in two batches.
4 Spread two-thirds of the mixture into pan. Top with apples, leaving a 2cm border around the edge; cover with remaining mixture.
5 Bake cake about 50 minutes. Stand cake in pan 5 minutes; turn, top-side up, onto wire rack to cool.
6 Meanwhile, return reserved apple liquid to large frying pan, add cream; bring to the boil. Reduce heat; simmer, uncovered, about 15 minutes or until sauce thickens.
7 Serve warm cake with caramel sauce.

preparation time 20 minutes
cooking time 1 hour **serves** 10
tip We used golden delicious apples in this recipe – a crisp, almost citrus-coloured apple with excellent flavour and good keeping properties. It's probably the best cooking apple around, but you can substitute it with green-skinned granny smiths, if you like.

Quince and blackberry crumble cake

185g butter, softened
¾ cup (165g) caster sugar
2 eggs
2¼ cups (335g) self-raising flour
¾ cup (180ml) milk
2 cups (300g) frozen blackberries
2 teaspoons cornflour
poached quince
3 cups (750ml) water
¾ cup (165g) caster sugar
1 cinnamon stick
1 tablespoon lemon juice
3 medium quinces (1kg), each cut into 8 wedges
cinnamon crumble
¾ cup (110g) plain flour
2 tablespoons caster sugar
½ cup (110g) firmly packed brown sugar
100g cold butter, chopped
1 teaspoon ground cinnamon

1 Make poached quince.
2 Preheat oven to 180°C/160°C fan-forced. Grease deep 23cm-square cake pan; line base and sides with baking paper.
3 Beat butter and sugar in small bowl with electric mixer until light and fluffy. Beat in eggs, one at a time. Transfer to large bowl; stir in sifted flour and milk, in two batches. Spread mixture into pan; bake 25 minutes.
4 Meanwhile, blend or process ingredients for cinnamon crumble, pulsing until ingredients just come together.
5 Remove cake from oven. Working quickly, toss frozen blackberries in cornflour to coat. Top cake with drained quince then blackberries; sprinkle crumble over fruit. Bake further 20 minutes. Stand cake in pan 5 minutes; turn, top-side up, onto wire rack. Serve with reserved quince syrup.
poached quince Stir the water, sugar, cinnamon stick and juice in medium saucepan over low heat until sugar dissolves. Add quince; bring to the boil. Reduce heat; simmer, covered, about 1½ hours or until quince is tender and rosy in colour. Cool quince in syrup to room temperature; strain quince over medium bowl. Reserve quince and syrup separately.
preparation time 30 minutes
cooking time 2 hours 15 minutes (plus cooling time) **serves** 16

Almond honey spice cake

125g butter, softened
⅓ cup (75g) caster sugar
2 tablespoons honey
1 teaspoon ground ginger
1 teaspoon ground allspice
2 eggs
1½ cups (180g) almond meal
½ cup (80g) semolina
1 teaspoon baking powder
¼ cup (60ml) milk
spiced syrup
1 cup (220g) caster sugar
1 cup (250ml) water
8 cardamom pods, bruised
2 cinnamon sticks
honey orange cream
¾ cup (180ml) thickened cream
1 tablespoon honey
2 tablespoons finely grated orange rind

1 Preheat oven to 180°C/160°C fan-forced. Grease deep 20cm-round cake pan; line base and side with baking paper.
2 Beat butter, sugar, honey and spices in small bowl with electric mixer until light and fluffy. Beat in eggs, one at a time. Transfer mixture to medium bowl; fold in almond meal, semolina, baking powder and milk.
3 Spread mixture into pan; bake about 40 minutes.
4 Meanwhile, make spiced syrup. Pour strained hot syrup over hot cake in pan; cool cake in pan to room temperature. Turn cake, in pan, upside-down onto serving plate; refrigerate 3 hours or overnight.
5 Remove cake from refrigerator. Make honey orange cream. Remove pan from cake; serve cake at room temperature with honey orange cream.
spiced syrup Stir ingredients in small saucepan over heat, without boiling, until sugar dissolves; bring to the boil. Boil, uncovered, without stirring, about 5 minutes or until syrup thickens slightly.
honey orange cream Beat cream, honey and rind in small bowl with electric mixer until soft peaks form.
preparation time 20 minutes
cooking time 40 minutes (plus cooling, refrigeration and standing time)
serves 8

Pineapple cake with coconut liqueur cream

1 cup (75g) shredded coconut
450g can crushed pineapple in syrup
125g butter, softened
½ cup (110g) caster sugar
2 eggs
1½ cups (225g) self-raising flour
6 egg whites
½ cup (110g) caster sugar, extra
2 teaspoons icing sugar
coconut liqueur cream
300ml thickened cream
¼ cup (40g) icing sugar
1 tablespoon coconut-flavoured liqueur

1 Toast coconut in medium frying pan, stirring constantly, 2 minutes or until browned lightly. Remove from pan; cool. Drain pineapple over small bowl; reserve ½ cup of the syrup, discard remainder.

2 Preheat oven to 180°C/160°C fan-forced. Grease two deep 20cm-round springform tins; line bases and sides with baking paper.

3 Beat butter and sugar in small bowl with electric mixer until light and fluffy. Beat in eggs, one at a time. Transfer mixture to large bowl; stir in sifted flour, pineapple, then reserved syrup. Divide mixture between tins; bake 20 minutes.

4 Meanwhile, beat egg whites in small bowl with electric mixer until soft peaks form; gradually add extra caster sugar, beating until sugar dissolves between additions. Fold in toasted coconut.

5 Remove cakes from oven. Working quickly; divide coconut mixture over cakes in tins, using spatula to spread evenly so tops are completely covered. Bake about 30 minutes. Stand cakes in tins 5 minutes; using small knife, carefully loosen meringue from baking paper around inside of tin. Release sides of tins; cool.

6 Meanwhile, make coconut liqueur cream.

7 Place one cake on serving plate; spread with cream. Top with remaining cake; dust with sifted icing sugar.

coconut liqueur cream Beat cream, sugar and liqueur in small bowl with electric mixer until soft peaks form.

preparation time 25 minutes
cooking time 50 minutes (plus cooling time) **serves** 10

Maple pecan cake

cooking-oil spray
1 cup (100g) pecans
⅓ cup (80ml) maple syrup
1¼ cups (235g) coarsely chopped dried figs
1 teaspoon bicarbonate of soda
1¼ cups (310ml) boiling water
60g butter
¾ cup (150g) firmly packed brown sugar
2 eggs
1 cup (150g) self-raising flour
maple butterscotch sauce
1 cup (250ml) maple syrup
½ cup (125ml) cream
100g butter, chopped

1 Preheat oven to 180°C/160°C fan-forced. Grease deep 20cm-round cake pan; line base with baking paper. Spray paper with oil.
2 Arrange nuts over base of pan; drizzle with maple syrup.
3 Place figs, soda and the water in bowl of food processor; cover with lid, stand 5 minutes. Add butter and sugar; process until almost smooth. Add eggs and flour; process until just combined. Pour mixture into pan.
4 Bake cake about 55 minutes. Stand cake in pan 5 minutes; turn onto wire rack to cool.
5 Meanwhile, make maple butterscotch sauce.
6 Serve cake with sauce and, if you like, vanilla ice-cream.
maple butterscotch sauce Stir ingredients in small saucepan over heat until smooth; bring to the boil. Boil, uncovered, about 2 minutes or until mixture thickens slightly.

preparation time 15 minutes
cooking time 1 hour **serves** 10
tip You can use either pure maple syrup or maple-flavoured syrup in this recipe.

Pear and almond cake with passionfruit glaze

You need about 4 passionfruit for this recipe.

185g butter, chopped
½ cup (110g) caster sugar
3 eggs
1½ cups (180g) almond meal
¼ cup (35g) plain flour
420g can pear halves in natural juice, drained
passionfruit glaze
⅓ cup (80ml) passionfruit pulp
⅓ cup (80ml) light corn syrup
1 tablespoon caster sugar

1 Make passionfruit glaze.
2 Preheat oven to 160°C/140°C fan-forced. Grease 22cm springform tin; line base and side with baking paper.
3 Beat butter and sugar in medium bowl with electric mixer until light and fluffy. Beat in eggs, one at a time; stir in almond meal and flour. Spread mixture into tin; top with pears.
4 Bake cake about 50 minutes. Stand cake in pan 5 minutes. Remove from tin; turn, top-side up, onto wire rack. Pour glaze over cake.
passionfruit glaze Stir combined ingredients in small saucepan over heat, without boiling, until sugar dissolves. Bring to the boil; reduce heat. Simmer, uncovered, without stirring, about 2 minutes or until thickened slightly; cool.

preparation time 30 minutes
cooking time 50 minutes **serves** 12
tips Canned pears generally hold their shape well when used in baking, and don't lose any of their sweet, juicy flavour.
Cake and glaze can be made a day ahead and refrigerated, covered separately, until required.

Warm apple cake with brandy butterscotch sauce

125g butter, chopped
½ cup (110g) caster sugar
2 eggs
⅔ cup (100g) self-raising flour
⅓ cup (50g) plain flour
1 tablespoon milk
3 medium granny smith apples (450g)
½ cup (160g) apricot jam, warmed
brandy butterscotch sauce
½ cup (100g) firmly packed brown sugar
½ cup (125ml) thickened cream
100g butter, chopped
2 tablespoons brandy

1 Preheat oven to 160°C/140°C fan-forced. Grease two 8cm x 25cm bar cake pans; line base and sides with baking paper.
2 Beat butter and sugar in small bowl with electric mixer until light and fluffy. Beat in eggs, one at a time; stir in sifted flours and milk. Divide mixture between pans.
3 Peel, core and halve apples; slice halves thinly. Push apple slices gently into surface of cake mixture. Brush apple with strained jam.
4 Bake cakes about 40 minutes. Stand cakes in pans 10 minutes; turn, top-side up, onto wire rack to cool.
5 Meanwhile, make brandy butterscotch sauce. Drizzle sauce over pieces of warm cake.
brandy butterscotch sauce Stir ingredients in small saucepan over heat, without boiling, until sugar dissolves; bring to the boil. Reduce heat; simmer, uncovered, without stirring, about 3 minutes or until mixture thickens slightly.

preparation time 30 minutes
cooking time 40 minutes **serves** 8
tip Peel, core and cut apples just before using to prevent the flesh browning. You could also use golden delicious apples in this recipe.

Cinnamon teacake

60g butter, softened
1 teaspoon vanilla extract
⅔ cup (150g) caster sugar
1 egg
1 cup (150g) self-raising flour
⅓ cup (80ml) milk
10g butter, melted, extra
1 teaspoon ground cinnamon
1 tablespoon caster sugar, extra

1 Preheat oven to 180°C/160°C fan-forced. Grease deep 20cm-round cake pan; line base with baking paper.
2 Beat butter, extract, sugar and egg until light and fluffy. Stir in sifted flour and milk. Spread mixture into pan.
3 Bake cake about 30 minutes. Stand cake in pan 5 minutes; turn, top-side up, onto wire rack. Brush top of cake with melted butter, sprinkle with combined cinnamon and extra sugar.

preparation time 15 minutes
cooking time 30 minutes **serves** 8
tip This cake can be stored in an airtight container for up to 2 days.

Greek yogurt cake

125g butter, softened
1 cup (220g) caster sugar
3 eggs, separated
2 cups (300g) self-raising flour
½ teaspoon bicarbonate of soda
¼ cup (40g) finely chopped blanched almonds
1 cup (280g) yogurt

1 Preheat oven to 180°C/160°C fan-forced. Grease 20cm x 30cm lamington pan; line base with baking paper, extending paper 5cm over long sides.
2 Beat butter and sugar in small bowl with electric mixer until light and fluffy. Beat in egg yolks. Transfer mixture to large bowl; stir in sifted flour and soda in two batches. Stir in nuts and yogurt.
3 Beat egg whites in small bowl with electric mixer until soft peaks form. Fold egg whites into yogurt mixture, in two batches. Spread mixture into pan.
4 Bake cake about 35 minutes. Turn cake, top-side up, onto wire rack to cool. Dust with sifted icing sugar, if you like.

preparation time 25 minutes
cooking time 35 minutes (plus cooling time) **serves** 12

Apricot chocolate chip cake

1 cup (150g) chopped dried apricots
1 cup (250ml) apricot nectar
125g butter, softened
²/₃ cup (150g) raw sugar
2 eggs, separated
1½ cups (120g) desiccated coconut
1½ cups (225g) self-raising flour
½ cup (95g) dark Choc Bits

1 Combine apricots and nectar in medium bowl; stand 1 hour.
2 Preheat oven to 180°C/160°C fan-forced. Grease deep 20cm-round cake pan; line base with baking paper.
3 Beat butter and sugar in small bowl with electric mixer until light and fluffy. Beat in egg yolks. Transfer mixture to large bowl; stir in coconut then sifted flour and apricot mixture, in two batches. Stir in Choc Bits.
4 Beat egg whites in small bowl with electric mixer until soft peaks form; fold into apricot mixture. Spread mixture into pan.
5 Bake cake about 1¼ hours. Stand cake in pan 10 minutes; turn, top-side up, onto wire rack to cool. Serve dusted with sifted icing sugar, if you like.

preparation time 30 minutes (plus standing time)
cooking time 1 hour 15 minutes (plus cooling time) **serves** 8
tip This cake can be stored in an airtight container for up to 3 days.

Moist coconut cake with coconut ice frosting

125g butter, softened
½ teaspoon coconut essence
1 cup (220g) caster sugar
2 eggs
½ cup (40g) desiccated coconut
1½ cups (225g) self-raising flour
300g sour cream
⅓ cup (80ml) milk
coconut ice frosting
2 cups (320g) icing sugar
1⅓ cups (110g) desiccated coconut
2 egg whites, beaten lightly
pink food colouring

1 Preheat oven to 180°C/160°C fan-forced. Grease deep 22cm-round cake pan; line base with baking paper.
2 Beat butter, essence and sugar in small bowl with electric mixer until light and fluffy. Beat in eggs, one at a time. Transfer mixture to large bowl; stir in coconut, sifted flour, sour cream and milk, in two batches. Spread mixture into pan.
3 Bake cake about 1 hour. Stand cake in pan 5 minutes; turn, top-side up, onto wire rack to cool.
4 Meanwhile, make coconut ice frosting.
5 Top cold cake with frosting; decorate with fresh raspberries if you like.
coconut ice frosting Sift icing sugar into medium bowl; stir in coconut and egg whites. Tint pink with a little colouring.

preparation time 25 minutes
cooking time 1 hour (plus cooling time) **serves** 10

Date, ricotta and polenta cake

1 cup (170g) finely chopped seeded dried dates
⅓ cup (80ml) orange-flavoured liqueur
2 cups (300g) self-raising flour
1 teaspoon baking powder
⅔ cup (110g) polenta
1 cup (220g) caster sugar
1¼ cups (250g) ricotta cheese
125g butter, melted
¾ cup (180ml) water
½ cup (75g) coarsely chopped roasted hazelnuts
ricotta filling
1¼ cups (250g) ricotta cheese
2 tablespoons orange-flavoured liqueur
2 tablespoons icing sugar
1 tablespoon finely grated orange rind

1 Preheat oven to 160°C/140°C fan-forced. Grease deep 22cm-round cake pan; line base and side with baking paper.
2 Combine dates and liqueur in small bowl; stand 15 minutes.
3 Meanwhile, make ricotta filling.
4 Beat flour, baking powder, polenta, sugar, ricotta, butter and the water in large bowl on low speed with electric mixer until combined. Increase speed to medium; beat until mixture changes to a paler colour. Stir in nuts and undrained date mixture.
5 Spread half the cake mixture into pan; spread ricotta filling over cake mixture. Spread with remaining cake mixture.
6 Bake cake about 45 minutes. Cover tightly with foil; bake further 1 hour. Discard foil, stand cake in pan 10 minutes; turn, top-side up, onto wire rack to cool.
ricotta filling Stir ingredients in medium bowl until smooth.

preparation time 30 minutes (plus standing time)
cooking time 1 hour 55 minutes (plus cooling time) **serves** 16

Apricot loaf

200g dried apricots, chopped coarsely
½ cup (125ml) apricot nectar
½ cup (110g) caster sugar
½ cup (110g) firmly packed brown sugar
250g butter, chopped
3 eggs
1 cup (150g) plain flour
¾ cup (110g) self-raising flour

1 Preheat oven to 150°C/130°C fan-forced. Grease 14cm x 21cm loaf pan; line base and long sides with baking paper, extending paper 2cm over sides.
2 Bring apricots, nectar and sugars to the boil in medium saucepan. reduce heat; simmer, covered, 5 minutes, stirring occasionally. Remove from heat; add butter, stir until melted. Transfer mixture to large bowl; cover, cool to room temperature.
3 Stir eggs and sifted flours into apricot mixture. Spread mixture into pan.
4 Bake loaf about 1¼ hours. Cover loaf with foil; cool in pan.

preparation time 15 minutes
cooking time 1 hour 25 minutes (plus cooling time) **serves** 8
tip This loaf can be stored, covered, in an airtight container for up to 2 days or frozen for up to 3 months.

Fig jam and raisin rolls

125g butter
½ cup (100g) firmly packed brown sugar
2 eggs
1½ cups (225g) self-raising flour
½ cup (160g) fig jam
1 cup (170g) chopped raisins
½ cup (125ml) milk

1 Preheat oven to 180°C/160°C fan-forced. Grease two 8cm x 19cm nut roll tins; line bases with baking paper. Place tins upright on oven tray.
2 Beat butter and sugar in small bowl with electric mixer until light and fluffy. Beat in eggs, one at a time. Transfer mixture to medium bowl; stir in flour, jam, raisins and milk, in two batches. Spoon mixture into tins; replace lids.
3 Bake rolls about 50 minutes. Stand rolls in tins 5 minutes; remove ends (top and bottom), shake tins gently to release rolls onto wire rack to cool.

preparation time 20 minutes
cooking time 50 minutes (plus cooling time) **serves** 20
tips Nut roll tins are available from cookware shops and department stores. There are different sizes and types of nut roll tins available, and it is important that you do not fill them with too much mixture. As a loose guide, the tins should be filled just a little over halfway. Some nut roll tins open along the side; be certain these are closed properly before baking. Some lids have tiny holes in them to allow steam to escape; make sure these are not used on the bottom of the tins. Well-cleaned fruit juice cans may be used instead of the nut roll tins; use a double thickness of foil as a substitute for the lids.
Store fruit rolls in an airtight container for up to 3 days or freeze for up to 3 months.

Passionfruit buttermilk cake

250g butter, softened
1 cup (220g) caster sugar
3 eggs, separated
2 cups (300g) self-raising flour
¾ cup (180ml) buttermilk
¼ cup (60ml) passionfruit pulp
passionfruit icing
1½ cups (240g) icing sugar
¼ cup (60ml) passionfruit pulp, approximately

1 Preheat oven to 180°C/160°C fan-forced. Grease and lightly flour 24cm bundt pan; tap out excess flour.
2 Beat butter and sugar in small bowl with electric mixer until light and fluffy. Beat in egg yolks, one at a time. Transfer mixture to large bowl; stir in sifted flour, buttermilk and passionfruit, in two batches.
3 Beat egg whites in small bowl with electric mixer until soft peaks form. Fold into cake mixture, in two batches. Spread mixture into pan.
4 Bake cake about 40 minutes. Stand cake in pan 5 minutes; turn onto wire rack to cool.
5 Meanwhile, make passionfruit icing; drizzle over cold cake.
passionfruit icing Sift icing sugar into small heatproof bowl; stir in enough passionfruit pulp to form a firm paste. Stand bowl over small saucepan of simmering water, stir until icing is a pouring consistency (do not overheat).

preparation time 20 minutes
cooking time 45 minutes (plus cooling time) **serves** 12
tips You could bake this cake in a deep 22cm-round cake pan; it will take about 1 hour to cook.
This cake is best made on the day of serving. Uniced cake can be frozen for up to 3 months.

Hummingbird cupcakes

You need 2 medium overripe bananas (460g) for this recipe.

440g can crushed pineapple in syrup
1 cup (160g) wholemeal plain flour
½ cup (80g) wholemeal self-raising flour
½ teaspoon bicarbonate of soda
½ teaspoon ground cinnamon
½ teaspoon ground ginger
1 cup (220g) firmly packed brown sugar
2 eggs, beaten lightly
¼ cup (20g) desiccated coconut
¾ cup mashed banana
⅓ cup (80ml) vegetable oil
½ cup (80g) icing sugar
2 tablespoons toasted shredded coconut

1 Preheat oven to 180°C/160°C fan-forced. Line 12-hole (⅓-cup/80ml) muffin pan with paper cases.
2 Drain pineapple over small bowl, pressing with spoon to extract as much syrup as possible. Reserve ⅓ cup of the syrup, discard remainder.
3 Sift flours, soda, spices and brown sugar into medium bowl. Stir in ¼ cup of the reserved syrup, egg, desiccated coconut, banana and oil. Divide mixture among paper cases.
4 Bake cupcakes about 25 minutes. Stand cakes in pan 5 minutes; turn, top-side up, onto wire rack to cool.
5 Meanwhile, place icing sugar in small bowl; add enough of the remaining syrup to make icing spreadable. Drizzle cupcakes with icing, sprinkle with shredded coconut.

preparation time 20 minutes
cooking time 25 minutes **makes** 12

Carrot cupcakes with maple frosting

You need 4 medium carrots (480g) for this recipe.

1½ cups (225g) self-raising flour
1 cup (220g) firmly packed brown sugar
2 teaspoons mixed spice
½ cup (125ml) vegetable oil
3 eggs
2 cups (480g) firmly packed coarsely grated carrot
¾ cup (90g) coarsely chopped roasted pecans
6 roasted pecans, halved
maple cream cheese frosting
30g butter, softened
80g cream cheese, softened
2 tablespoons maple syrup
1¼ cups (200g) icing sugar

1 Preheat oven to 180°C/160°C fan-forced. Line 12-hole (⅓-cup/80ml) muffin pan with paper cases.
2 Combine sifted flour, sugar, spice, oil and eggs in medium bowl. Stir in carrot and chopped nuts. Divide mixture among paper cases.
3 Bake cupcakes about 30 minutes. Stand cakes in pan 5 minutes; turn, top-side up, onto wire rack to cool.
4 Meanwhile, make maple cream cheese frosting.
5 Spread frosting over cupcakes; top each with a nut.
maple cream cheese frosting Beat butter, cream cheese and syrup in small bowl with electric mixer until light and fluffy; gradually beat in sifted icing sugar until spreadable.

preparation time 30 minutes (plus cooling time)
cooking time 30 minutes **makes** 12

Cupcakes

125g butter, softened
1 teaspoon vanilla extract
⅔ cup (150g) caster sugar
3 eggs
1½ cups (225g) self-raising flour
¼ cup (60ml) milk
glacé icing
1½ cups (240g) icing sugar
1 teaspoon butter, softened
2 tablespoons milk, approximately
food colouring, optional

1 Preheat oven to 180°C/160°C fan-forced. Line two deep 12-hole patty pans with paper cases.
2 Beat butter, extract, sugar, eggs, flour and milk in small bowl of electric mixer on low speed until ingredients are just combined. Increase speed to medium, beat about 3 minutes or until mixture is smooth and changed to a paler colour. Drop slightly rounded tablespoons of mixture into paper cases.
3 Bake cupcakes about 20 minutes. Turn cakes, top-side up, onto wire racks to cool.
4 Meanwhile, make glacé icing. Spread icing over cold cupcakes.
glacé icing Place icing sugar in small heatproof bowl, stir in butter and enough milk to give a firm paste. Add a few drops of food colouring, if you like. Stir over a small saucepan of simmering water until icing is spreadable; do not overheat.

variation
butterfly cakes Using sharp pointed vegetable knife, cut circle from top of each cake; cut circle in half to make two "wings". Divide ½ cup (160g) of your favourite jam and 300ml whipped cream among cavities. Place wings in position on top of cakes; top with strawberry pieces and dust with a little sifted icing sugar, if you like.

preparation time 15 minutes
cooking time 25 minutes (plus cooling time) **makes** 24
tips Cakes are at their best made on day of serving. Unfilled and uniced cakes can be frozen for up to 1 month. Cream-filled cakes should be refrigerated if made more than an hour ahead. Use two paper cases in each patty pan hole for added stability when making butterfly cakes.

Rock cakes

2 cups (300g) self-raising flour
¼ teaspoon ground cinnamon
⅓ cup (75g) caster sugar
90g butter, chopped
1 cup (160g) sultanas
1 egg, beaten lightly
½ cup (125ml) milk
1 tablespoon caster sugar, extra

1 Preheat oven to 200°C/180°C fan-forced. Grease oven trays.
2 Sift flour, cinnamon and sugar into medium bowl; rub in butter with fingertips. Stir in sultanas, egg and milk. Do not over-mix.
3 Drop rounded tablespoons of mixture about 5cm apart onto trays; sprinkle with extra sugar.
4 Bake cakes about 15 minutes; cool on trays.

variations
cranberry and fig Substitute caster sugar with ⅓ cup firmly packed brown sugar. Omit sultanas; stir 1 cup coarsely chopped dried figs and ¼ cup dried cranberries into mixture before egg and milk are added.
pineapple, lime and coconut Omit sultanas; stir 1 cup coarsely chopped dried pineapple, ¼ cup toasted flaked coconut and 1 teaspoon finely grated lime rind into mixture before egg and milk are added.

preparation time 15 minutes
cooking time 15 minutes **makes** 18
tip Rock cakes can be stored in an airtight container for up to 2 days.

Rhubarb and almond cakes

½ cup (125ml) milk
¼ cup (40g) blanched almonds, roasted
80g butter, softened
1 teaspoon vanilla extract
½ cup (110g) caster sugar
2 eggs
1 cup (150g) self-raising flour
poached rhubarb
250g trimmed rhubarb, chopped coarsely
¼ cup (60ml) water
½ cup (110g) white sugar

1 Preheat oven to 180°C/160°C fan-forced. Grease a 6-hole texas
(¾-cup/180ml) muffin pan.
2 Make poached rhubarb.
3 Meanwhile, blend or process milk and nuts until smooth.
4 Beat butter, extract and sugar in small bowl with electric mixer until
light and fluffy. Beat in eggs, one at a time. Transfer mixture to large bowl;
stir in sifted flour and almond mixture. Divide mixture among pan holes.
5 Bake cakes 10 minutes. Carefully remove pan from oven; divide
drained rhubarb among cakes, bake further 15 minutes. Stand cakes in
pan 5 minutes; turn, top-side up, onto wire rack.
6 Serve cakes warm or cold with reserved rhubarb syrup.
poached rhubarb Stir ingredients in medium saucepan over medium
heat; bring to the boil. Reduce heat; simmer, uncovered, about 10 minutes
or until rhubarb is just tender. Drain rhubarb over medium bowl; reserve
rhubarb and syrup separately.

preparation time 20 minutes
cooking time 40 minutes **makes** 6
tip Be sure to discard every bit of the rhubarb's leaf and use only the
thinnest stalks (the thick ones tend to be stringy).

Mini chocolate hazelnut cakes

100g dark eating chocolate, chopped coarsely
¾ cup (180ml) water
100g butter, softened
1 cup (220g) firmly packed brown sugar
3 eggs
¼ cup (25g) cocoa powder
¾ cup (110g) self-raising flour
⅓ cup (35g) hazelnut meal
whipped hazelnut ganache
⅓ cup (80ml) thickened cream
180g milk eating chocolate, chopped finely
2 tablespoons hazelnut-flavoured liqueur

1 Preheat oven to 180°C/160°C fan-forced. Grease 12 x ½-cup (125ml) oval friand pans.
2 Make whipped hazelnut ganache.
3 Meanwhile, stir chocolate and the water in medium saucepan over low heat until smooth.
4 Beat butter and sugar in small bowl with electric mixer until light and fluffy. Beat in eggs, one at a time (mixture may curdle at this stage, but will come together later); transfer mixture to medium bowl. Stir in warm chocolate mixture, sifted cocoa and flour, and hazelnut meal. Divide mixture among pans.
5 Bake cakes about 20 minutes. Stand cakes in pans 5 minutes; turn, top-sides up, onto wire rack to cool. Spread ganache over cakes.
whipped hazelnut ganache Stir cream and chocolate in small saucepan over low heat until smooth. Stir in liqueur; transfer mixture to small bowl. Cover; stand about 2 hours or until just firm. Beat ganache in small bowl with electric mixer until mixture changes to a pale brown colour.

preparation time 35 minutes
cooking time 25 minutes (plus standing time) **makes** 12

Gluten-free berry cupcakes

125g butter, softened
2 teaspoons finely grated lemon rind
¾ cup (165g) caster sugar
4 eggs
2 cups (240g) almond meal
½ cup (40g) desiccated coconut
½ cup (100g) rice flour
1 teaspoon bicarbonate of soda
1 cup (150g) frozen mixed berries
1 tablespoon desiccated coconut, extra

1 Preheat oven to 180°C/160°C fan-forced. Grease 12-hole (⅓-cup/ 80ml) muffin pan.
2 Beat butter, rind and sugar in small bowl with electric mixer until light and fluffy. Beat in eggs, one at a time (mixture may curdle at this stage, but will come together later). Transfer mixture to large bowl; stir in almond meal, coconut, sifted flour and soda, then berries. Divide mixture among pan holes.
3 Bake cupcakes about 25 minutes. Stand cupcakes in pan 5 minutes; turn, top-sides up, onto wire rack to cool. Sprinkle with extra coconut.

preparation time 20 minutes
cooking time 25 minutes **makes** 12

Coffee caramel cakes

125g butter, softened
⅔ cup (150g) firmly packed brown sugar
2 tablespoons instant coffee granules
1 tablespoon boiling water
2 eggs
2 cups (300g) self-raising flour
½ cup (125ml) milk
18 (130g) jersey caramels, halved

1 Preheat oven to 180°C/160°C fan-forced. Grease 12-hole (⅓-cup/80ml) muffin pan.
2 Beat butter and sugar in small bowl with electric mixer until light and fluffy. Add combined coffee and the water; beat in eggs, one at a time. Transfer mixture to large bowl; stir in sifted flour and milk.
3 Spoon mixture into pan holes. Press 3 caramel halves into the centre of each cake; cover with batter.
4 Bake cakes about 20 minutes. Stand cakes in pan 5 minutes; turn, top-side up, onto wire racks to cool.

preparation time 15 minutes
cooking time 20 minutes (plus cooling time) **makes** 12
tips Jersey caramels are available in supermarkets and chain stores, they are on the soft side, caramel in colour with a white stripe in the middle. These cakes are best made on day of serving. Cakes suitable to freeze for up to 1 month.

Buttery apple cinnamon cakes

125g butter, softened
1 teaspoon vanilla extract
¾ cup (165g) caster sugar
2 eggs
¾ cup (110g) self-raising flour
¼ cup (35g) plain flour
⅓ cup (80ml) apple juice
1 small red apple (130g)
1½ tablespoons demerara sugar
¼ teaspoon ground cinnamon

1 Preheat oven to 180°C/160°C fan-forced. Grease 8-hole (½-cup/
125ml) petite loaf pan.
2 Beat butter, extract and caster sugar in small bowl with electric mixer
until light and fluffy. Beat in eggs, one at a time. Transfer mixture to
medium bowl; fold in combined sifted flours and juice, in two batches.
Spread mixture into pan holes.
3 Cut the unpeeled apple into quarters; remove core, slice thinly. Overlap
apple slices on top of cakes.
4 Combine demerara sugar and cinnamon in small bowl; sprinkle half
the sugar mixture over cakes.
5 Bake cakes about 25 minutes. Turn cakes, top-side up, onto wire rack
to cool. Sprinkle with remaining sugar mixture.

preparation time 10 minutes
cooking time 25 minutes (plus cooling time) **makes** 8
tips These cakes can be stored in airtight container for up to 3 days or
frozen for up to 3 months.
The cake mixture can also be cooked in texas muffin pan.

Orange syrup cakes

3 medium oranges (720g)
250g butter, chopped coarsely
1½ cups (330g) caster sugar
4 eggs
¾ cup (120g) semolina
¾ cup (90g) almond meal
¾ cup (110g) self-raising flour
orange syrup
1 medium orange (240g)
½ cup (110g) caster sugar
1 cup (250ml) water

1 Preheat oven to 160°C/140°C fan-forced. Line two 12-hole (⅓-cup/80ml) muffin pans with paper cases.
2 Coarsely chop oranges, including skin; remove and discard seeds. Place oranges in medium saucepan, add enough boiling water to cover. Bring to the boil, simmer, uncovered, about 15 minutes or until tender; cool. Drain oranges, then blend or process until smooth.
3 Beat butter and sugar in small bowl with electric mixer until light and fluffy. Beat in eggs, one at a time. Transfer mixture to large bowl; stir in semolina, almond meal and sifted flour, then orange puree. Spoon mixture into paper cases.
4 Bake cakes about 40 minutes.
5 Meanwhile, make orange syrup.
6 Place hot cakes on wire rack over oven tray. Pour hot syrup over hot cakes. Serve warm or cold.
orange syrup Peel rind thinly from orange, avoiding any white pith. Cut rind into thin strips. Stir sugar and the water in small saucepan over low heat, without boiling, until sugar is dissolved. Bring syrup to the boil; add rind, simmer, uncovered, 5 minutes. Transfer syrup to a heatproof jug.

preparation time 25 minutes
cooking time 1 hour 10 minutes (plus cooling time) **makes** 24
tip These cakes can be made 4 days ahead. Not suitable to freeze.

Gingerbread loaves

200g butter, softened
1¼ cups (275g) caster sugar
¾ cup (270g) treacle
2 eggs
3 cups (450g) plain flour
1½ tablespoons ground ginger
3 teaspoons mixed spice
1 teaspoon bicarbonate of soda
¾ cup (180ml) milk
vanilla icing
3 cups (500g) icing sugar
2 teaspoons butter, softened
½ teaspoon vanilla extract
⅓ cup (80ml) milk

1 Preheat oven to 180°C/160°C fan-forced. Grease two 8-hole (½-cup/125ml) petite loaf pans.
2 Beat butter and sugar in small bowl with electric mixer until light and fluffy. Add treacle, beat 3 minutes. Beat in eggs, one at a time. Transfer mixture to large bowl; stir in sifted dry ingredients, then milk, in two batches. Divide mixture between pans.
3 Bake loaves about 25 minutes. Stand loaves in pans 5 minutes; turn, top-side up, onto wire rack to cool.
4 Meanwhile, make vanilla icing; spread over loaves.
vanilla icing Sift icing sugar into heatproof bowl; stir in butter, extract and milk to form a smooth paste. Place bowl over simmering water; stir until spreadable.

preparation time 35 minutes
cooking time 25 minutes (plus cooling time) **makes** 16
tips You could also bake this recipe in two 12-hole (⅓-cup/80ml) muffin pans; line 22 holes with paper cases.
These cakes can be stored in an airtight container for up to 4 days.
Uniced cakes can be frozen for up to 3 months.

Raspberry hazelnut cake

250g butter, softened
2 cups (440g) caster sugar
6 eggs
1 cup (150g) plain flour
½ cup (75g) self-raising flour
1 cup (100g) hazelnut meal
⅔ cup (160g) sour cream
300g fresh or frozen raspberries
¼ cup (35g) roasted hazelnuts, chopped coarsely
mascarpone cream
1 cup (250g) mascarpone cheese
¼ cup (40g) icing sugar
2 tablespoons hazelnut-flavoured liqueur
½ cup (120g) sour cream

1 Preheat oven to 180°C/160°C fan-forced. Grease deep 22cm-round cake pan; line base and side with baking paper.
2 Beat butter and sugar in medium bowl with electric mixer until light and fluffy. Beat in eggs, one at a time (mixture will curdle at this stage, but will come together later). Transfer mixture to large bowl; stir in sifted flours, hazelnut meal, sour cream and raspberries. Spread mixture into pan.
3 Bake cake about 1½ hours. Stand cake in pan 10 minutes; turn, top-side up, onto wire rack to cool.
4 Meanwhile, make mascarpone cream.
5 Spread mascarpone cream all over cold cake, top with nuts.
mascarpone cream Stir ingredients in medium bowl until smooth.

preparation time 30 minutes
cooking time 1 hour 30 minutes (plus cooling time) **serves** 12
tips If using frozen raspberries, don't thaw them; frozen berries are less likely to "bleed" into the cake mixture.
We used Frangelico, but you can use any hazelnut-flavoured liqueur.
Unfrosted cake will keep for up to 3 days in an airtight container at room temperature. Cake can be frosted the day before required; store, covered, in refrigerator. Unfrosted cake can be frozen for up to 3 months.

Apple ginger cakes with lemon icing

You need 1 large apple (200g) for this recipe.

250g butter, softened
1½ cups (330g) firmly packed dark brown sugar
3 eggs
¼ cup (90g) golden syrup
2 cups (300g) plain flour
1½ teaspoons bicarbonate of soda
2 tablespoons ground ginger
1 tablespoon ground cinnamon
1 cup (170g) coarsely grated apple
⅔ cup (160ml) hot water
lemon icing
2 cups (320g) icing sugar
2 teaspoons butter, softened
⅓ cup (80ml) lemon juice

1 Preheat oven to 180°C/160°C fan-forced. Grease two 6-hole mini fluted tube pans.
2 Beat butter and sugar in small bowl with electric mixer until light and fluffy. Beat in eggs, one at a time. Stir in syrup. Transfer mixture to medium bowl; stir in sifted dry ingredients, then apple and the water. Divide mixture among pans; smooth surface.
3 Bake cakes about 25 minutes. Stand cakes in pan 5 minutes; turn, top-side down, onto wire racks to cool.
4 Meanwhile, make lemon icing; drizzle icing over warm cakes.
lemon icing Sift icing sugar into small heatproof bowl; stir in butter and juice to form a paste. Place bowl over small saucepan of simmering water; stir until icing is a pouring consistency.

preparation time 15 minutes
cooking time 25 minutes (plus cooling time) **makes** 12
tips You can also make these cakes in 6-hole texas (¾-cup/180ml) muffin pans lined with paper cases.
These cakes can be stored in an airtight container for up to 3 days.
Uniced cakes can be frozen for up to 3 months.

biscuits

Chocolate melting moments

125g butter, softened
2 tablespoons icing sugar
¾ cup (110g) plain flour
2 tablespoons cornflour
1 tablespoon cocoa powder
¼ cup (85g) chocolate hazelnut spread

1 Preheat oven to 180°C/160°C fan-forced. Grease oven trays; line with baking paper.
2 Beat butter and sifted icing sugar in small bowl with electric mixer until light and fluffy. Stir in sifted dry ingredients.
3 Spoon mixture into piping bag fitted with 1cm-fluted tube. Pipe stars about 3cm apart on trays.
4 Bake biscuits about 10 minutes. Cool on trays.
5 Sandwich biscuits with hazelnut spread.

preparation time 15 minutes
cooking time 10 minutes (plus cooling time) **makes** 20
tip Melting moments can be stored in an airtight container for up to 1 week.

Orange hazelnut butter yoyo bites

250g butter, softened, chopped
1 teaspoon vanilla extract
½ cup (80g) icing sugar
1½ cups (225g) plain flour
½ cup (75g) cornflour
orange hazelnut butter
80g butter, softened
2 teaspoons finely grated orange rind
⅔ cup (110g) icing sugar
1 tablespoon hazelnut meal

1 Preheat oven to 160°C/140°C fan-forced. Grease oven trays; line with baking paper.
2 Beat butter, extract and sifted icing sugar in small bowl with electric mixer until light and fluffy; stir in sifted flours, in two batches.
3 Roll rounded teaspoons of mixture into balls; place about 3cm apart on trays. Using fork dusted with flour, press tines gently onto each biscuit to flatten slightly.
4 Bake biscuits about 15 minutes. Cool on trays.
5 Meanwhile, make orange hazelnut butter.
6 Sandwich biscuits with orange hazelnut butter. Serve bites dusted with extra sifted icing sugar, if you like.
orange hazelnut butter Beat butter, rind and sifted icing sugar in small bowl with electric mixer until light and fluffy. Stir in hazelnut meal.

preparation time 15 minutes
cooking time 15 minutes (plus cooling time) **makes** 20
tip Yoyo bites can be stored in an airtight container for up to 1 week.

Vanilla kisses

125g butter, softened
½ cup (110g) caster sugar
1 egg
⅓ cup (50g) plain flour
¼ cup (35g) self-raising flour
⅔ cup (100g) cornflour
¼ cup (30g) custard powder
vienna cream
60g butter, softened
½ teaspoon vanilla extract
¾ cup (120g) icing sugar
2 teaspoons milk

1 Preheat oven to 200°C/180°C fan-forced. Grease oven trays; line with baking paper.
2 Beat butter, sugar and egg in small bowl with electric mixer until light and fluffy. Stir in sifted dry ingredients, in two batches.
3 Spoon mixture into piping bag fitted with 1cm-fluted tube. Pipe 3cm rosettes about 3cm apart on trays.
4 Bake biscuits about 10 minutes. Cool on trays.
5 Meanwhile, make vienna cream.
6 Sandwich biscuits with vienna cream.
vienna cream Beat butter and extract in small bowl with electric mixer until as white as possible; gradually beat in sifted icing sugar and milk, in two batches.

preparation time 15 minutes
cooking time 10 minutes (plus cooling time) **makes** 20
tip Kisses can be stored in an airtight container for up to 1 week.

Coffee hazelnut meringues

2 egg whites
½ cup (110g) caster sugar
2 teaspoons instant coffee granules
½ teaspoon hot water
3 teaspoons coffee-flavoured liqueur
¼ cup (35g) roasted hazelnuts

1 Preheat oven to 120°C/100°C fan-forced. Grease oven trays; line with baking paper.
2 Beat egg whites in small bowl with electric mixer until soft peaks form. Gradually add sugar, beating until dissolved between additions.
3 Meanwhile, dissolve coffee in the water in small jug; stir in liqueur. Fold coffee mixture into meringue mixture.
4 Spoon mixture into piping bag fitted with 5mm fluted tube. Pipe meringues onto trays 2cm apart; top each meringue with a nut.
5 Bake meringues about 45 minutes. Cool in oven with door ajar.

preparation time 10 minutes
cooking time 45 minutes (plus cooling time) **makes** 30
tip Meringues can be stored in an airtight container for up to 3 weeks. Suitable to freeze for up to 3 months.

Coconut macaroons

1 egg, separated
1 egg yolk
¼ cup (55g) caster sugar
1⅔ cups (120g) shredded coconut

1 Preheat oven to 150°C/130°C fan-forced. Grease oven trays; line with baking paper.
2 Beat egg yolks and sugar in small bowl until creamy; stir in coconut.
3 Beat egg white in small bowl until firm peaks form; stir gently into coconut mixture. Drop heaped teaspoons of the mixture onto trays.
4 Bake macaroons about 15 minutes.
5 Reduce oven to 120°C/100°C fan-forced; bake further 30 minutes or until biscuits are golden brown. Loosen biscuits while warm; cool on trays.

preparation time 15 minutes
cooking time 45 minutes **makes** 18
tips Macaroons can be stored in an airtight container for up to 3 weeks. Suitable to freeze for up to 3 months.

Honey jumbles

60g butter
½ cup (110g) firmly packed brown sugar
¾ cup (270g) golden syrup
1 egg, beaten lightly
2½ cups (375g) plain flour
½ cup (75g) self-raising flour
½ teaspoon bicarbonate of soda
1 teaspoon ground cinnamon
½ teaspoon ground clove
2 teaspoons ground ginger
1 teaspoon mixed spice
icing
1 egg white
1½ cups (240g) icing sugar
2 teaspoons plain flour
1 tablespoon lemon juice, approximately
pink food colouring

1 Stir butter, sugar and syrup in medium saucepan over low heat until sugar dissolves; cool 10 minutes. Transfer mixture to large bowl; stir in egg and sifted dry ingredients, in two batches. Knead dough on floured surface until dough loses stickiness. Cover; refrigerate 30 minutes.
2 Preheat oven to 160°C/140°C fan-forced. Grease oven trays; line with baking paper.
3 Divide dough into eight portions. Roll each portion into 2cm-thick sausage; cut each sausage into five 6cm lengths. Place about 3cm apart on oven trays; round ends using floured fingers, flatten slightly.
4 Bake biscuits about 15 minutes. Cool on trays.
5 Meanwhile, make icing.
6 Spread jumbles with pink and white icing.
icing Beat egg white lightly in small bowl; gradually stir in sifted icing sugar and flour, then enough juice to make icing spreadable. Place half the mixture in another small bowl; tint with colouring. Keep icings covered with a damp tea towel.

preparation time 10 minutes (plus refrigeration time)
cooking time 15 minutes (plus cooling time) **makes** 40
tip Jumbles can be stored in an airtight container for up to 1 week.

Anzac biscuits

1 cup (90g) rolled oats
1 cup (150g) plain flour
1 cup (220g) caster sugar
¾ cup (60g) desiccated coconut
125g butter, chopped
1 tablespoon golden syrup
1½ teaspoons bicarbonate of soda
2 tablespoons boiling water

1 Preheat oven to 150°C/130°C fan-forced. Grease oven trays; line with baking paper.
2 Combine oats, flour, sugar and coconut in large bowl.
3 Stir butter and syrup in small saucepan over low heat until smooth.
4 Combine soda and the boiling water in small heatproof bowl, add to butter mixture; stir into dry ingredients while warm.
5 Place level tablespoons of mixture onto trays about 5cm apart; press lightly.
6 Bake biscuits about 25 minutes. Loosen biscuits while warm; cool on trays.

preparation time 30 minutes
cooking time 25 minutes **makes** 25
tip Biscuits can be stored in an airtight container for up to 2 weeks.

Banana, date and rolled oat cookies

You need 1 medium overripe banana (230g) for this recipe.

125g butter, softened
1 teaspoon finely grated lemon rind
1 cup (220g) firmly packed brown sugar
1 egg yolk
⅓ cup mashed banana
1½ cups (225g) plain flour
½ teaspoon bicarbonate of soda
1 cup (90g) rolled oats
½ cup (75g) finely chopped seeded dried dates
⅔ cup (60g) rolled oats, extra
4 dried dates (35g), seeded, chopped coarsely

1 Preheat oven to 180°C/160°C fan-forced. Grease oven trays; line with baking paper.
2 Beat butter, rind, sugar and egg yolk in small bowl with electric mixer until combined; stir in banana then sifted flour and soda, oats and dates.
3 Roll level tablespoons of mixture into balls; roll each ball in extra oats then place on trays 5cm apart. Press a piece of coarsely chopped date into centre of each ball.
4 Bake cookies about 15 minutes. Cool on trays.

preparation time 20 minutes
cooking time 15 minutes **makes** 28
tips Biscuits can be stored in an airtight container for up to 3 weeks. Suitable to freeze for up to 3 months.

Lemon shortbreads

250g butter, softened, chopped
1 teaspoon finely grated lemon rind
⅓ cup (55g) icing sugar
1½ cups (225g) plain flour
½ cup (75g) cornflour
½ cup (85g) mixed peel, chopped finely

1 Preheat oven to 180°C/160°C fan-forced. Grease oven trays.
2 Beat butter, rind and sifted icing sugar in small bowl with electric mixer until just changed in colour. Stir in sifted flours, in two batches.
3 Place mixture into large piping bag fitted with fluted tube, pipe mixture into rosettes, about 2cm apart, onto trays; sprinkle with mixed peel.
4 Bake biscuits about 15 minutes or until browned lightly. Stand biscuits on tray 10 minutes; transfer to wire racks to cool.

preparation time 20 minutes
cooking time 15 minutes **makes** 40
tips Shortbreads can be stored in an airtight container for up to 3 weeks. Suitable to freeze for up to 3 months.

Macadamia shortbread

250g butter, softened, chopped
½ cup (110g) caster sugar
2 teaspoons vanilla extract
2 cups (300g) plain flour
½ cup (75g) rice flour
½ cup (75g) finely chopped macadamias
2 tablespoons caster sugar, extra

1 Preheat oven to 160°C/140°C fan-forced. Grease two oven trays.
2 Beat butter, sugar and extract in small bowl with electric mixer until pale and fluffy. Transfer mixture to large bowl; stir in sifted flours and nuts, in two batches. Knead on floured surface until smooth.
3 Divide mixture into two portions; roll each portion, between sheets of baking paper, into 23cm circle. Press an upturned 22cm loose-based fluted flan tin into shortbread to cut rounds. Cut each round into 12 wedges. Place on trays; mark with a fork, sprinkle with extra sugar.
4 Bake shortbread about 20 minutes or until a pale straw colour. Stand on tray 10 minutes; transfer to wire rack to cool.

preparation time 20 minutes
cooking time 20 minutes (plus cooling time) **makes** 24
tips Shortbread can be stored in an airtight container for up to 3 weeks. Suitable to freeze for up to 3 months.

Traditional shortbread

250g butter, softened
⅓ cup (75g) caster sugar
1 tablespoon water
2 cups (300g) plain flour
½ cup (100g) rice flour
2 tablespoons white sugar

1 Preheat oven to 160°C/140°C fan-forced. Grease two oven trays.
2 Beat butter and caster sugar in medium bowl with electric mixer until light and fluffy; stir in the water and sifted flours, in two batches. Knead on floured surface until smooth.
3 Divide mixture in two portions; shape each portion, on separate trays, into 20cm rounds. Mark each round into 12 wedges; prick with fork. Pinch edges of rounds with fingers; sprinkle with white sugar.
4 Bake shortbread about 40 minutes. Stand on trays 5 minutes. Using sharp knife, cut into wedges along marked lines. Cool on trays.

variations
lemon squares Beat 1 tablespoon finely grated lemon rind into the butter and sugar mixture. Shape dough into a 30cm x 4cm rectangular log, cut into 1cm slices. Place about 3cm apart on oven trays; sprinkle with 2 tablespoons raw sugar. Bake about 20 minutes. Stand 5 minutes; place onto wire racks to cool. Makes 24
pistachio and white chocolate mounds Roast ½ cup unsalted pistachios; chop two-thirds finely, reserve remainder. Fold chopped pistachios and 100g finely chopped white eating chocolate into basic shortbread mixture before flours are added. Shape level tablespoons of mixture into mounds; place about 3cm apart on oven trays, press a reserved nut into each mound. Bake about 20 minutes. Stand 5 minutes; place onto wire racks to cool. Serve dusted with icing sugar. Makes 32

preparation time 20 minutes
cooking time 40 minutes **makes** 24
tips Shortbread can be stored in an airtight container for up to 3 weeks. Suitable to freeze for up to 3 months.

Anise-flavoured shortbread

250g butter, softened
½ cup (80g) icing sugar
2 cups (300g) plain flour
½ cup (100g) rice flour
3 teaspoons ground aniseed

1 Beat butter and sifted icing sugar in medium bowl with electric mixer until light and fluffy. Add sifted flours and aniseed, in two batches, beating on low speed after each addition, only until combined. Knead on floured surface until smooth. Cover; refrigerate 1 hour.
2 Preheat oven to 160°C/140°C fan-forced. Grease three oven trays; line with baking paper.
3 Roll dough between sheets of baking paper until 5mm thick. Cut 36 x 6cm flower shapes or rounds from dough; place on oven trays about 3cm apart. Refrigerate 15 minutes.
4 Bake biscuits about 12 minutes. Cool on trays.

preparation time 20 minutes (plus refrigeration time)
cooking time 12 minutes **makes** 36
tips Biscuits can be stored in an airtight container for up to 3 weeks. Suitable to freeze for up to 3 months.

Almond and chocolate florentines

50g butter
¼ cup (55g) caster sugar
2 teaspoons honey
1 tablespoon plain flour
1 tablespoon cream
½ cup (40g) flaked almonds
50g dark eating chocolate, melted

1 Preheat oven to 200°C/180°C fan-forced. Grease four oven trays;
line with baking paper.
2 Combine butter, sugar, honey, flour and cream in small saucepan;
bring to the boil, stirring. Reduce heat; cook, without stirring, 2 minutes.
Remove from heat; stir in nuts.
3 Drop level teaspoons of mixture about 8cm apart onto trays.
4 Bake florentines about 6 minutes or until golden brown. Remove
from oven; using metal spatula, push florentines into rounds. Cool on
trays 1 minute then carefully lift florentines onto baking-paper-covered
wire rack to cool.
5 Drizzle florentines with chocolate; refrigerate until set.

preparation time 20 minutes (plus refrigeration time)
cooking time 6 minutes (plus cooling time) **makes** 28
tips Florentines can be stored in an airtight container for up to 2 weeks.
Not suitable to freeze.

White chocolate macadamia cookies

1½ cups (225g) plain flour
½ teaspoon bicarbonate of soda
¼ cup (55g) caster sugar
⅓ cup (75g) firmly packed brown sugar
125g butter, melted
½ teaspoon vanilla extract
1 egg
180g white eating chocolate, chopped coarsely
¾ cup (105g) roasted macadamias, chopped coarsely

1 Preheat oven to 200°C/180°C fan-forced. Grease two oven trays; line with baking paper.
2 Sift flour, soda and sugars into large bowl. Stir in butter, extract and egg then chocolate and nuts.
3 Drop rounded tablespoons of mixture, 5cm apart on trays.
4 Bake cookies about 10 minutes. Cool on trays.

preparation time 10 minutes
cooking time 10 minutes **makes** 24
tips Cookies can be stored in an airtight container for up to 3 weeks. Suitable to freeze for up to 3 months.

White choc, apple and almond bread

3 egg whites
⅓ cup (75g) caster sugar
¾ cup (110g) plain flour
¼ teaspoon ground cinnamon
⅔ cup (110g) whole blanched almonds
1 cup (55g) finely chopped dried apples
50g white eating chocolate, melted

1 Preheat oven to 180°C/160°C fan-forced. Grease 8cm x 26cm bar cake pan; line base and two long sides with baking paper, extending paper 5cm over edges.
2 Beat egg whites and sugar in small bowl with electric mixer until sugar dissolves. Fold in sifted flour then cinnamon, nuts and apple. Spread mixture into pan.
3 Bake bread about 30 minutes. Stand bread in pan 10 minutes; turn, top-side up, onto wire rack to cool.
4 Reduce oven temperature to 150°C/130°C fan-forced.
5 Using serrated knife, slice cooled bread thinly; place slices on ungreased oven trays. Bake about 15 minutes or until crisp. Turn onto wire rack to cool. Drizzle biscuits with chocolate.

preparation time 10 minutes
cooking time 1 hour (plus cooling time) **makes** 50
tip Almond bread can be stored in an airtight container for up to 4 weeks.

Hazelnut biscotti

1⅓ cups (200g) plain flour
⅓ cup (50g) self-raising flour
1 cup (220g) caster sugar
2 eggs, beaten lightly
½ cup (75g) roasted hazelnuts
1 teaspoon vanilla extract

1 Preheat oven to 180°C/160°C fan-forced. Grease oven tray.
2 Sift flours and sugar into large bowl. Stir in egg, nuts and extract until mixture becomes a firm dough.
3 Knead dough on floured surface until mixture just comes together; shape mixture into 25cm log, place on tray.
4 Bake log about 35 minutes or until firm. Cool on tray.
5 Reduce oven temperature to 150°C/130°C fan-forced.
6 Using a serrated knife, cut log diagonally into 5mm slices. Place slices, in single layer, on ungreased oven trays. Bake about 10 minutes or until dry and crisp, turning over halfway through cooking; transfer to wire racks to cool.

preparation time 40 minutes
cooking time 45 minutes (plus cooling time) **makes** 50
tip Biscotti can be stored in an airtight container for up to 4 weeks.

Choc nut biscotti

2 eggs
1 cup (220g) caster sugar
1⅔ cups (250g) plain flour
1 teaspoon baking powder
1 cup (150g) roasted pistachios
½ cup (70g) slivered almonds
¼ cup (25g) cocoa powder

1 Preheat oven to 180°C/160°C fan-forced. Grease oven tray.
2 Whisk eggs and sugar in medium bowl. Stir in sifted flour, baking powder and nuts; mix to a sticky dough.
3 Knead dough on floured surface until smooth. Divide dough into two portions. Using floured hands, knead one portion on floured surface until smooth, but still slightly sticky. Divide this portion into four pieces; roll each piece into 25cm log shape.
4 Knead cocoa into remaining portion of dough until smooth. Divide chocolate dough into two pieces; roll each piece into 25cm log shape.
5 Place one chocolate log on tray. Place a plain log on each side, press gently together to form a slightly flattened shape. Repeat with remaining logs.
6 Bake logs about 30 minutes. Cool on tray 10 minutes.
7 Reduce oven to 150°C/130°C fan-forced.
8 Using a serrated knife, cut logs diagonally into 5mm slices. Place slices, in single layer, on ungreased oven trays. Bake about 20 minutes or until dry and crisp, turning over halfway through cooking; transfer to wire racks to cool.

preparation time 35 minutes
cooking time 50 minutes (plus cooling time) **makes** 100
tip Biscotti can be stored in an airtight container for up to 4 weeks.

Apricot and pine nut biscotti

2 eggs
1¼ cups (275g) caster sugar
1 teaspoon vanilla extract
1½ cups (225g) plain flour
½ cup (75g) self-raising flour
½ cup (125g) coarsely chopped glacé apricots
¼ cup (40g) roasted pine nuts
2 teaspoons water

1 Preheat oven to 180°C/160°C fan-forced. Grease oven tray.
2 Whisk eggs, sugar and extract in medium bowl. Stir in sifted flours, apricots, pine nuts and the water; mix to a sticky dough. Knead dough on floured surface until smooth.
3 Divide dough into two portions. Using floured hands, roll each portion into a 30cm log. Place logs on tray.
4 Bake logs about 25 minutes. Cool on tray 10 minutes.
5 Reduce oven to 150°C/130°C fan-forced.
6 Using a serrated knife, cut logs diagonally into 1cm slices. Place slices, in single layer, on ungreased oven trays. Bake about 25 minutes or until dry and crisp, turning over halfway through cooking; transfer to wire racks to cool.

preparation time 25 minutes
cooking time 50 minutes (plus cooling time) **makes** 60
tip Biscotti can be stored in an airtight container for up to 4 weeks.

Orange, coconut and almond biscotti

2 eggs
1 cup (220g) caster sugar
1 teaspoon grated orange rind
1⅓ cups (200g) plain flour
⅓ cup (50g) self-raising flour
⅔ cup (50g) shredded coconut
1 cup (160g) blanched almonds

1 Preheat oven to 180°C/160°C fan-forced. Grease oven tray.
2 Whisk eggs, sugar and rind together in medium bowl. Stir in sifted flours, coconut and nuts; mix to a sticky dough.
3 Knead dough on floured surface until smooth. Divide dough into two portions. Using floured hands, roll each portion into a 20cm log; place logs on tray.
4 Bake logs about 35 minutes. Cool on tray 10 minutes.
5 Reduce oven to 150°C/130°C fan-forced.
6 Using a serrated knife, cut logs diagonally into 1cm slices. Place slices, in single layer, on ungreased oven trays. Bake about 25 minutes or until dry and crisp, turning over halfway through cooking; transfer to wire racks to cool.

preparation time 25 minutes
cooking time 1 hour (plus cooling time) **makes** 40
tip Biscotti can be stored in an airtight container for up to 4 weeks.

Pistachio and cranberry biscotti

60g butter, softened
1 teaspoon vanilla extract
1 cup (220g) caster sugar
2 eggs
1¾ cups (260g) plain flour
½ teaspoon bicarbonate of soda
1 cup (130g) dried cranberries
¾ cup (110g) coarsely chopped roasted pistachios
1 egg, extra
1 tablespoon water
2 tablespoons caster sugar, extra

1 Beat butter, extract and sugar in medium bowl until combined. Beat in eggs, one at a time. Stir in sifted flour and soda then cranberries and nuts. Cover dough; refrigerate 1 hour.
2 Preheat oven to 180°C/160°C fan-forced. Grease oven tray.
3 Knead dough on floured surface until smooth but still sticky. Halve dough; shape each half into 30cm log. Place logs on oven tray.
4 Combine extra egg with the water in small bowl. Brush egg mixture over logs; sprinkle with extra sugar.
5 Bake logs about 20 minutes or until firm; cool 3 hours or overnight.
6 Preheat oven to 150°C/130°C fan-forced.
7 Using serrated knife, cut logs diagonally into 1cm slices. Place slices, in single layer, on ungreased oven trays. Bake about 15 minutes or until dry and crisp, turning halfway through cooking time; transfer to wire racks to cool.

preparation time 20 minutes (plus refrigeration time)
cooking time 40 minutes (plus cooling time) **makes** 60
tip Biscotti can be stored in an airtight container for up to 4 weeks.

Gingernuts

90g butter
⅓ cup (75g) firmly packed brown sugar
⅓ cup (115g) golden syrup
1⅓ cups (200g) plain flour
¾ teaspoon bicarbonate of soda
1 tablespoon ground ginger
1 teaspoon ground cinnamon
¼ teaspoon ground clove

1 Preheat oven to 180°C/160°C fan-forced. Grease oven trays; line with baking paper.
2 Stir butter, sugar and syrup in medium saucepan over low heat until smooth. Remove from heat; stir in sifted dry ingredients. Cool 10 minutes.
3 Roll rounded teaspoons of mixture into balls. Place about 3cm apart on trays; flatten slightly.
4 Bake biscuits about 10 minutes. Cool on trays.

preparation time 15 minutes
cooking time 10 minutes (plus cooling time) **makes** 32
tips Biscuits can be stored in an airtight container for up to 3 weeks. Suitable to freeze for up to 3 months.

Crunchy muesli cookies

1 cup (90g) rolled oats
1 cup (150g) plain flour
1 cup (220g) caster sugar
2 teaspoons ground cinnamon
¼ cup (35g) dried cranberries
⅓ cup (55g) finely chopped dried apricots
½ cup (70g) slivered almonds
125g butter, chopped coarsely
2 tablespoons golden syrup
½ teaspoon bicarbonate of soda
1 tablespoon boiling water

1 Preheat oven 150°C/130°C fan-forced. Grease oven trays; line with
baking paper.
2 Combine oats, flour, sugar, cinnamon, dried fruit and nuts in large bowl.
3 Melt butter with golden syrup in small saucepan over low heat;
add combined soda and the boiling water. Stir warm butter mixture
into dry ingredients.
4 Roll level tablespoons of mixture into balls, place on trays 5cm apart;
flatten slightly.
5 Bake cookies about 20 minutes. Cool on trays.

preparation time 15 minutes
cooking time 25 minutes **makes** 36
tips Cookies can be stored in an airtight container for up to 3 weeks.
Suitable to freeze for up to 3 months.

Hazelnut pinwheels

1¼ cups (185g) plain flour
100g butter, chopped coarsely
½ cup (110g) caster sugar
1 egg yolk
1 tablespoon milk, approximately
⅓ cup (110g) chocolate hazelnut spread
2 tablespoons hazelnut meal

1 Process flour, butter and sugar until crumbly. Add egg yolk; process with enough milk until mixture forms a ball. Knead dough on floured surface until smooth; cover, refrigerate 1 hour.
2 Roll dough between sheets of baking paper to form 20cm x 30cm rectangle; remove top sheet of paper. Spread dough evenly with chocolate hazelnut spread; sprinkle with hazelnut meal. Using paper as a guide, roll dough tightly from long side to enclose filling. Enclose roll in plastic wrap; refrigerate 30 minutes.
3 Preheat oven to 180°C/160°C fan-forced. Grease oven trays; line with baking paper.
4 Remove plastic from dough; cut roll into 1cm slices. Place slices about 2cm apart on trays.
5 Bake biscuits about 20 minutes. Stand biscuits on trays 5 minutes; transfer to wire rack to cool.

preparation time 20 minutes (plus refrigeration time)
cooking time 20 minutes **makes** 30
tips Pinwheels can be stored in an airtight container for up to 3 weeks. Suitable to freeze for up to 3 months.

Frangipane jam drops

125g butter, softened
½ teaspoon vanilla extract
½ cup (110g) caster sugar
1 cup (120g) almond meal
1 egg
⅔ cup (100g) plain flour
2 tablespoons raspberry jam

1 Preheat oven to 180°C/160°C fan forced. Grease oven trays;
line with baking paper.
2 Beat butter, extract, sugar and almond meal in small bowl with
electric mixer until light and fluffy. Beat in egg until just combined;
stir in sifted flour.
3 Drop level tablespoons of mixture on trays 5cm apart. Use handle
of wooden spoon to make small hole (about 1cm deep) in top of each
biscuit; fill each hole with ¼ teaspoon jam.
4 Bake jam drops about 15 minutes. Cool on trays.

preparation time 30 minutes
cooking time 15 minutes **makes** 24
tips Jam drops can be stored in an airtight container for up to 3 weeks.
Suitable to freeze for up to 3 months.

Vanilla bean thins

1 vanilla bean
30g butter, softened
¼ cup (55g) caster sugar
1 egg white, beaten lightly
¼ cup (35g) plain flour

1 Preheat oven to 200°C/180°C fan-forced. Grease oven trays;
line with baking paper.
2 Halve vanilla bean lengthways; scrape seeds into medium bowl,
discard pod. Add butter and sugar to bowl; stir until combined. Stir
in egg white and flour.
3 Spoon mixture into piping bag fitted with 5mm plain tube. Pipe
6cm-long strips (making them slightly wider at both ends) about 5cm
apart on trays.
4 Bake biscuits about 5 minutes or until edges are browned lightly.
Cool on trays.

preparation time 20 minutes
cooking time 5 minutes **makes** 24
tip Biscuits can be stored in an airtight container for up to 1 week.

Golden pecan twists

⅓ cup (40g) finely chopped pecans
2 tablespoons golden syrup
125g butter, softened
¼ teaspoon vanilla extract
⅓ cup (75g) caster sugar
1 egg yolk
1 cup (150g) plain flour

1 Preheat oven to 180°C/160°C fan-forced. Grease oven trays; line with baking paper.
2 Combine nuts and half of the golden syrup in small bowl.
3 Beat butter, extract, sugar, egg yolk and remaining golden syrup in small bowl with electric mixer until light and fluffy. Stir in sifted flour.
4 Shape rounded teaspoons of mixture into balls; roll each ball into 12cm log. Twist each log into a loop, overlapping one end over the other. Place twists on trays 3cm apart; top each twist with ½ teaspoon nut mixture.
5 Bake twists about 10 minutes. Cool on trays.

preparation time 25 minutes
cooking time 10 minutes **makes** 30
tips Twists can be stored in an airtight container for up to 3 weeks. Suitable to freeze for up to 3 months.
Finely chopped walnuts, hazelnuts or macadamias can be used instead of pecans, if you prefer.

Coffee almond biscuits

1 tablespoon instant coffee granules
3 teaspoons hot water
3 cups (360g) almond meal
1 cup (220g) caster sugar
2 tablespoons coffee-flavoured liqueur
3 egg whites, beaten lightly
24 coffee beans

1 Preheat oven to 180°C/160°C fan-forced. Grease oven trays;
line with baking paper.
2 Dissolve coffee in the hot water in large bowl. Add almond meal,
sugar, liqueur and egg whites; stir until mixture forms a firm paste.
3 Roll level tablespoons of mixture into balls, place on trays 3cm apart;
flatten slightly. Press coffee beans into tops of biscuits.
4 Bake biscuits about 15 minutes. Cool on trays.

preparation time 15 minutes
cooking time 15 minutes **makes** 24
tips Biscuits can be stored in an airtight container for up to 3 weeks.
Suitable to freeze for up to 3 months.

Oat and bran biscuits

1 cup (150g) plain flour
1 cup (60g) unprocessed bran
¾ cup (60g) rolled oats
½ teaspoon bicarbonate of soda
60g cold butter, chopped
½ cup (110g) caster sugar
1 egg
2 tablespoons water, approximately

1 Process flour, bran, oats, soda and butter until crumbly; add sugar, egg and enough of the water to make a firm dough. Knead dough on floured surface until smooth. Cover; refrigerate 30 minutes.
2 Preheat oven to 180°C/160°C fan-forced. Grease oven trays; line with baking paper.
3 Divide dough in half; roll each half between sheets of baking paper to about 5mm thickness. Cut dough into 7cm rounds; place rounds on trays about 2cm apart.
4 Bake biscuits about 15 minutes. Stand biscuits on trays 5 minutes; transfer to wire rack to cool.

preparation time 15 minutes (plus refrigeration time)
cooking time 15 minutes **makes** 30
tips Biscuits can be stored in an airtight container for up to 3 weeks. Suitable to freeze for up to 3 months.
Use traditional rolled oats for this recipe, not the instant variety.

Triple-choc cookies

125g butter, softened
½ teaspoon vanilla extract
1¼ cups (250g) firmly packed brown sugar
1 egg
1 cup (150g) plain flour
¼ cup (35g) self-raising flour
1 teaspoon bicarbonate of soda
⅓ cup (35g) cocoa powder
½ cup (85g) chopped raisins
½ cup (95g) milk Choc Bits
½ cup (75g) white chocolate Melts, halved
½ cup (75g) dark chocolate Melts, halved

1 Preheat oven to 180°C/160°C fan-forced. Grease two oven trays; line with baking paper.
2 Beat butter, extract, sugar and egg in small bowl with electric mixer until smooth; do not overbeat. Stir in sifted dry ingredients, then raisins and all chocolates.
3 Drop level tablespoons of mixture onto trays about 5cm apart.
4 Bake cookies about 10 minutes. Stand cookies on trays 5 minutes; transfer to wire rack to cool.

preparation time 10 minutes
cooking time 10 minutes **makes** 36
tips For a firmer cookie, bake an extra 2 minutes.
Cookies can be stored in an airtight container for up to 3 weeks.
Suitable to freeze for up to 3 months.

Maple-syrup butter cookies

125g butter, softened
½ teaspoon vanilla extract
⅓ cup (80ml) maple syrup
¾ cup (110g) plain flour
¼ cup (35g) cornflour

1 Preheat oven to 180°C/160°C fan-forced. Grease oven trays;
line with baking paper.
2 Beat butter, extract and maple syrup in small bowl with electric mixer
until light and fluffy; stir in sifted flours.
3 Spoon mixture into piping bag fitted with 1cm fluted tube. Pipe stars
about 3cm apart onto trays.
4 Bake cookies about 15 minutes. Cool on trays.

preparation time 20 minutes
cooking time 15 minutes **makes** 24
tips Cookies can be stored in an airtight container for up to 3 weeks.
Suitable to freeze for up to 3 months.

Polenta and orange biscuits

125g butter, softened
2 teaspoons finely grated orange rind
⅔ cup (110g) icing sugar
⅓ cup (55g) polenta
1 cup (150g) plain flour

1 Preheat oven to 180°C/160°C fan-forced. Grease oven trays;
line with baking paper.
2 Beat butter, rind and sifted icing sugar in small bowl with electric mixer
until just combined; stir in polenta and sifted flour.
3 Shape mixture into 30cm-rectangular log; cut log into 1cm slices.
Place slices on trays 2cm apart.
4 Bake biscuits about 15 minutes. Stand biscuits on trays 5 minutes;
transfer to wire rack to cool.

preparation time 15 minutes
cooking time 15 minutes **makes** 30
tips Biscuits can be stored in an airtight container for up to 3 weeks.
Suitable to freeze for up to 3 months.

Chunky chocolate-chip cookies

125g butter, softened
1 teaspoon vanilla extract
1¼ cups (275g) firmly packed brown sugar
1 egg
1 cup (150g) plain flour
¼ cup (35g) self-raising flour
½ teaspoon bicarbonate of soda
⅓ cup (35g) cocoa powder
½ cup (100g) peanut M&M's
⅓ cup (70g) mini M&M's
½ cup (75g) milk chocolate Melts

1 Preheat oven to 180°C/160°C fan-forced. Grease two oven trays; line with baking paper.
2 Beat butter, extract, sugar and egg in small bowl with electric mixer until smooth (do not overmix). Transfer mixture to large bowl; stir in sifted dry ingredients then all chocolates.
3 Drop level tablespoons of mixture onto trays about 5cm apart.
4 Bake cookies about 10 minutes. Stand cookies on trays 5 minutes; transfer to wire rack to cool.

preparation time 20 minutes
cooking time 10 minutes **makes** 36
tips Biscuits can be stored in an airtight container for up to 3 weeks. Suitable to freeze for up to 3 months.

Passionfruit butter yoyo bites

250g butter, softened, chopped
1 teaspoon vanilla extract
½ cup (80g) icing sugar
1½ cups (225g) plain flour
½ cup (75g) cornflour
passionfruit butter
80g butter, softened
⅔ cup (150g) icing sugar
1 tablespoon passionfruit pulp

1 Preheat oven to 160°C/140°C fan-forced. Grease two oven trays; line with baking paper.
2 Beat butter, extract and sugar in medium bowl with electric mixer until light and fluffy. Stir in sifted dry ingredients, in two batches.
3 Roll rounded teaspoons of mixture into balls; place on trays about 3cm apart. Using fork dusted with a little flour, press tines gently onto each biscuit to flatten slightly.
4 Bake biscuits about 12 minutes or until firm. Stand on trays 5 minutes; transfer to wire rack to cool.
5 Meanwhile, make passionfruit butter.
6 Sandwich cool biscuits with passionfruit butter.
passionfruit butter Beat butter and sugar in small bowl with electric mixer until light and fluffy; stir in passionfruit pulp.

preparation time 20 minutes
cooking time 12 minutes (plus cooling time) **makes** 37
tip Biscuits can be stored in an airtight container for up to 1 week.

Amaretti

1 cup (120g) almond meal
1 cup (220g) caster sugar
2 egg whites
¼ teaspoon almond essence
20 blanched almonds (20g)

1 Grease two oven trays; line with baking paper.
2 Beat almond meal, sugar, egg whites and essence in small bowl with electric mixer for 3 minutes; stand 5 minutes.
3 Spoon mixture into piping bag fitted with 1cm plain tube. Pipe onto trays in circular motion from centre out, to make biscuits about 4cm in diameter. Top each biscuit with a nut. Cover trays of unbaked biscuits loosely with foil; stand at room temperature overnight.
4 Preheat oven to 180°C/160°C fan-forced.
5 Bake biscuits about 12 minutes. Stand on trays 5 minutes; transfer to wire rack to cool.

preparation time 15 minutes (plus standing time)
cooking time 12 minutes **makes** 20
tip Amaretti can be baked the day they're made, however, they will spread a little more. For best results, stand the amaretti overnight.

Greek-style almond biscuits

3 cups (375g) almond meal
1 cup (220g) caster sugar
¼ teaspoon almond essence
3 egg whites, beaten lightly
1 cup (80g) flaked almonds

1 Preheat oven to 180°C/160°C fan-forced. Grease two oven trays; line with baking paper.
2 Combine almond meal, sugar and essence in large bowl; stir in egg whites until mixture forms a firm paste.
3 Roll level tablespoons of mixture through nuts; roll into 8cm logs. Shape logs to form crescents. Place crescents on trays.
4 Bake biscuits about 15 minutes. Stand on trays 5 minutes; transfer to wire rack to cool.

preparation time 30 minutes
cooking time 15 minutes **makes** 25
tips Biscuits can be stored in an airtight container for up to 3 weeks. Suitable to freeze for up to 3 months.

Pistachio shortbread mounds

⅔ cup (90g) roasted pistachios
250g butter, softened
1 cup (160g) icing sugar
1½ cups (225g) plain flour
2 tablespoons rice flour
2 tablespoons cornflour
¾ cup (90g) almond meal
⅓ cup (55g) icing sugar, extra

1 Preheat oven to 150°C/130°C fan-forced. Grease two oven trays;
line with baking paper.
2 Coarsely chop half the nuts; leave remaining nuts whole.
3 Beat butter and sugar in small bowl with electric mixer until light and
fluffy. Transfer mixture to large bowl; stir in sifted flours, almond meal
and chopped nuts.
4 Shape level tablespoons of mixture into mounds; place on trays
about 3cm apart. Press one whole nut on each mound.
5 Bake mounds about 25 minutes or until firm. Stand mounds on
trays 5 minutes; transfer to wire rack to cool. Serve mounds dusted
with extra sifted icing sugar.

preparation time 25 minutes
cooking time 25 minutes **makes** 35
tips Biscuits can be stored in an airtight container for up to 3 weeks.
Suitable to freeze for up to 3 months.

Almond crisps

125g butter, softened
¼ cup (55g) caster sugar
1 cup (150g) self-raising flour
¼ cup (30g) almond meal
2 tablespoons flaked almonds

1 Preheat oven to 200°C/180°C fan-forced. Grease oven trays;
line with baking paper.
2 Beat butter and sugar in small bowl with electric mixer until smooth.
Stir in flour and almond meal.
3 Roll level tablespoons of mixture into balls; place onto trays about
5cm apart. Flatten slightly with a floured fork to 1cm thick; sprinkle
with flaked almonds.
4 Bake crisps about 10 minutes or until browned. Stand crisps on
trays 5 minutes; transfer to wire racks to cool.

preparation time 25 minutes
cooking time 10 minutes **makes** 15
tip Biscuits can be stored in an airtight container for up to 2 weeks.

Chunky chewy choc-chip cookies

1 cup (220g) firmly packed brown sugar
½ cup (110g) caster sugar
1½ cups (225g) self-raising flour
½ cup (75g) plain flour
1 cup (150g) coarsely chopped roasted macadamias
185g butter, melted, cooled
1 egg, beaten lightly
1 egg yolk, beaten lightly
2 teaspoons vanilla extract
200g dark eating chocolate, chopped coarsely

1 Preheat oven to 180°C/160°C fan-forced. Grease oven trays;
line with baking paper.
2 Combine sugars, sifted flours and nuts in large bowl. Add combined
butter, egg, egg yolk and extract; mix to a soft dough. Stir in chocolate.
3 Place 2 level tablespoons of biscuit dough on trays about 6cm apart.
4 Bake cookies about 16 minutes or until browned lightly. Cool on trays.

preparation time 25 minutes
cooking time 16 minutes **makes** 20
tips We used an ice-cream scoop equivalent to two level tablespoons
when measuring the biscuit dough.
Biscuits can be stored in an airtight container for up to 2 weeks.
Suitable to freeze for up to 3 months.

Chocolate lace crisps

100g dark eating chocolate, chopped coarsely
80g butter, chopped coarsely
1 cup (220g) caster sugar
1 egg
1 cup (150g) plain flour
2 tablespoons cocoa powder
¼ teaspoon bicarbonate of soda
¼ cup (40g) icing sugar

1 Melt chocolate and butter in small saucepan over low heat.
2 Transfer chocolate mixture to medium bowl; stir in caster sugar, egg and sifted flour, cocoa and soda. Cover; refrigerate about 15 minutes or until mixture is firm enough to handle.
3 Preheat oven to 180°C/160°C fan-forced. Grease oven trays; line with baking paper.
4 Roll level tablespoons of mixture into balls, roll each ball in icing sugar; place on trays 8cm apart.
5 Bake crisps about 15 minutes. Cool on trays.

preparation time 25 minutes (plus refrigeration time)
cooking time 20 minutes **makes** 24
tip Biscuits can be stored in an airtight container for up to 1 week.

Gingerbread kids

125g butter, chopped
⅓ cup (75g) firmly packed brown sugar
½ cup (175g) golden syrup
3 cups (450g) plain flour
2 teaspoons ground ginger
2 teaspoons ground cinnamon
½ teaspoon ground clove
2 teaspoons bicarbonate of soda
1 egg, beaten lightly
1 teaspoon vanilla extract
royal icing
1 egg white
1 cup (160g) pure icing sugar
food colourings

1 Preheat oven to 180°C/160°C fan-forced. Grease oven trays; line with baking paper.
2 Stir butter, sugar and golden syrup in small saucepan over low heat until butter has melted. Remove from heat; cool 5 minutes.
3 Sift combined flour, spices and soda into large bowl; stir in butter mixture, egg and extract.
4 Knead dough lightly on floured surface; roll dough to 5mm thickness. Using gingerbread-man cutter, cut out shapes; place on trays.
5 Bake gingerbread kids about 10 minutes or until golden brown. Cool on trays.
6 Meanwhile, make royal icing. Decorate gingerbread kids as you like with royal icing.
royal icing Beat egg white in small bowl with electric mixer until just frothy; gradually add sifted icing sugar, beating between additions, until stiff peaks form. Tint with food colourings as desired.

preparation time 30 minutes
cooking time 10 minutes (plus cooling time) **makes** 20
tips If the mixture in step 3 is dry and crumbly, add a little more beaten egg. You can use any shape of decorative cutter for this recipe.
Biscuits can be stored in an airtight container for up to 3 weeks.
Uniced biscuits suitable to freeze for up to 3 months.

Fudgy-wudgy chocolate cookies

125g butter, softened
1 teaspoon vanilla extract
1¼ cups (275g) firmly packed brown sugar
1 egg
1 cup (150g) plain flour
¼ cup (35g) self-raising flour
1 teaspoon bicarbonate of soda
⅓ cup (35g) cocoa powder
½ cup (75g) raisins
¾ cup (110g) roasted macadamias, chopped coarsely
½ cup (95g) dark Choc Bits
½ cup (75g) dark chocolate Melts, halved

1 Preheat oven to 180°C/160°C fan-forced. Line three oven trays with baking paper.
2 Beat butter, extract, sugar and egg in medium bowl with electric mixer until smooth. Stir in sifted flours, soda and cocoa powder; stir in raisins, nuts and both chocolates.
3 Drop rounded tablespoons of mixture onto trays about 4cm apart; flatten slightly.
4 Bake cookies 10 minutes. Stand cookies on trays 5 minutes; transfer to wire rack to cool.

preparation time 15 minutes
cooking time 10 minutes **makes** 24
tips Cookies can be stored in an airtight container for up to 3 weeks. Suitable to freeze for up to 3 months.
Other nuts, such as walnuts or pecans, can be used instead of macadamias.

Snickerdoodles

250g butter, softened
1 teaspoon vanilla extract
½ cup (110g) firmly packed brown sugar
1 cup (220g) caster sugar
2 eggs
2¾ cups (410g) plain flour
1 teaspoon bicarbonate of soda
½ teaspoon ground nutmeg
1 tablespoon caster sugar, extra
2 teaspoons ground cinnamon

1 Beat butter, extract and sugars in small bowl with electric mixer until light and fluffy. Beat in eggs, one at a time. Transfer mixture to large bowl; stir in combined sifted flour, soda and nutmeg, in two batches. Cover; refrigerate 30 minutes.
2 Preheat oven to 180°C/160°C fan-forced.
3 Combine extra caster sugar and cinnamon in small shallow bowl. Roll level tablespoons of the dough into balls; roll balls in cinnamon sugar. Place balls 7cm apart on ungreased oven trays.
4 Bake snickerdoodles about 12 minutes. Cool on trays.

preparation time 25 minutes (plus refrigeration time)
cooking time 12 minutes **makes** 50
tips Snickerdoodles can be stored in an airtight container for up to 3 weeks. Suitable to freeze for up to 3 months.

slices

No-bowl chocolate nut slice

90g butter, melted
1 cup (100g) plain sweet biscuit crumbs
1½ cups (285g) dark Choc Bits
1 cup (70g) shredded coconut
1 cup (140g) crushed mixed nuts
395g can sweetened condensed milk

1 Preheat oven to 180°C/160°C fan-forced. Grease 23cm-square slab pan; line base with baking paper extending paper 5cm over two opposite sides.
2 Pour butter into pan; sprinkle evenly with biscuit crumbs, Choc Bits, coconut and nuts. Drizzle with condensed milk.
3 Bake slice about 30 minutes. Cool in pan before cutting into pieces.

preparation time 10 minutes
cooking time 30 minutes (plus cooling time) **makes** about 18
tip This slice can be stored, covered, in the refrigerator for up to 1 week.

Chocolate hazelnut slice

250g plain chocolate biscuits
60g butter, melted
4 eggs, separated
¾ cup (165g) caster sugar
½ cup (50g) hazelnut meal
2 tablespoons plain flour
1 tablespoon cocoa powder
topping
125g butter, softened
½ cup (110g) caster sugar
1 tablespoon orange juice
200g dark eating chocolate, melted

1 Preheat oven to 180°C/160°C fan-forced. Grease 20cm x 30cm lamington pan; line base with baking paper, extending paper 5cm over long sides.
2 Process biscuits until fine. Combine 1 cup of the biscuit crumbs with butter in medium bowl; press over base of pan. Refrigerate 10 minutes.
3 Beat egg whites in small bowl with electric mixer until soft peaks form. Gradually add sugar, beating until dissolved between additions; fold in hazelnut meal, remaining biscuit crumbs and flour. Spread mixture over biscuit base.
4 Bake slice 20 minutes. Cool in pan 20 minutes.
5 Reduce oven to 170°C/150°C fan-forced.
6 Meanwhile, make topping; spead over slice.
7 Bake slice further 20 minutes. Cool in pan. Refrigerate until firm; dust with sifted cocoa before cutting.
topping Beat butter, sugar, egg yolks and juice in small bowl with electric mixer until light and fluffy. Stir in cooled chocolate.

preparation time 30 minutes
cooking time 40 minutes (plus cooling and refrigeration time)
makes 24

Fruity almond pistachio slice

¾ cup (180ml) sweetened condensed milk
125g butter, chopped
2 teaspoons grated lemon rind
1½ cups (150g) plain sweet biscuit crumbs
½ cup (125g) coarsely chopped red glacé cherries
½ cup (150g) coarsely chopped glacé figs
½ cup (125g) coarsely chopped glacé peaches
⅓ cup (55g) coarsely chopped roasted almonds
⅓ cup (50g) coarsely chopped roasted pistachios
¾ cup (65g) desiccated coconut
100g dark eating chocolate, melted
60g butter, melted, extra
1 tablespoon coarsely chopped roasted almonds, extra
1 tablespoon coarsely chopped roasted pistachios, extra

1 Grease 19cm x 29cm slice pan; line base with baking paper, extending paper 5cm over long sides.
2 Stir condensed milk, butter and rind in medium saucepan over heat until butter is melted. Stir in biscuit crumbs, fruit, nuts and coconut. Press mixture evenly over base of pan.
3 Spread with combined chocolate and extra butter, sprinkle with extra nuts; refrigerate until set.

preparation time 35 minutes
cooking time 5 minutes (plus refrigeration time) **makes** about 24
tip This slice can be stored, covered, in the refrigerator for up to 1 week.

Sweet coconut slice

1 cup (150g) plain flour
½ cup (75g) self-raising flour
2 tablespoons caster sugar
125g cold butter, chopped
1 egg
1 tablespoon iced water
½ cup (160g) apricot jam
10 red glacé cherries, halved
coconut filling
1 cup (220g) caster sugar
1 cup (250ml) water
3½ cups (280g) desiccated coconut
3 eggs, beaten lightly
60g butter, melted
¼ cup (60ml) milk
1 teaspoon vanilla extract
1 teaspoon baking powder

1 Process flours, sugar and butter until combined. Add egg and the water, process until mixture forms a ball; cover, refrigerate 30 minutes.
2 Meanwhile, make coconut filling.
3 Preheat oven to 180°C/160°C fan-forced. Line 25cm x 30cm swiss roll pan with baking paper, extending paper 5cm over long sides.
4 Roll pastry between sheets of baking paper until 3mm thick and large enough to cover base of pan. Gently ease into base of pan.
5 Brush jam evenly over pastry base. Spread coconut mixture over jam. Place cherry halves evenly over slice top.
6 Bake slice about 35 minutes. Cool in pan before cutting.
coconut filling Stir sugar and the water in small saucepan over heat until sugar is dissolved. Bring to the boil; boil 3 minutes without stirring. Cool 5 minutes. Place coconut in large bowl, stir in sugar syrup, egg, butter, milk, extract and baking powder.

preparation time 40 minutes (plus refrigeration time)
cooking time 40 minutes (plus cooling time) **makes** 20
tips This slice can be stored in an airtight container for up to 4 days. Cooked slice is suitable to freeze, covered, for up to 2 weeks. Thaw at room temperature.

Fruit chews

90g butter, chopped coarsely
⅓ cup (75g) firmly packed brown sugar
1¼ cups (185g) plain flour
1 egg yolk
topping
2 eggs
1 cup (220g) firmly packed brown sugar
⅓ cup (50g) self-raising flour
½ cup (85g) coarsely chopped raisins
¾ cup (120g) sultanas
1¼ cups (185g) roasted unsalted peanuts
1 cup (90g) desiccated coconut

1 Preheat oven to 180°C/160°C fan-forced. Grease 20cm x 30cm lamington pan; line base with baking paper, extending paper 5cm over long sides.
2 Stir butter and sugar in medium saucepan over medium heat until butter is melted. Stir in sifted flour and egg yolk. Press mixture over base of pan.
3 Bake base about 10 minutes or until browned lightly; cool.
4 Meanwhile, make topping; spread over cold base.
5 Bake slice about 30 minutes. Cool in pan before cutting.
topping Beat eggs and sugar in small bowl with electric mixer until changed to a paler colour and thickened slightly; stir in sifted flour. Transfer mixture to medium bowl; stir in remaining ingredients.

preparation time 15 minutes
cooking time 40 minutes (plus cooling time) **makes** 18
tips Brown sugar gives this nutty slice the colour and taste of caramel. This slice can be stored in an airtight container for up to 1 week.

Choc-cherry macaroon slice

3 egg whites
½ cup (110g) caster sugar
100g dark eating chocolate, grated coarsely
¼ cup (35g) plain flour
1⅓ cups (95g) shredded coconut, toasted
¾ cup (150g) glacé cherries, chopped coarsely
50g dark eating chocolate, melted

1 Preheat oven to 150°C/130°C fan-forced. Grease 19cm x 29cm slice
pan; line with baking paper, extending paper 5cm over long sides.
2 Beat egg whites in small bowl with electric mixer until soft peaks form;
gradually add sugar, beating until dissolved between additions. Fold in
grated chocolate, flour, coconut and cherries. Spread mixture into pan.
3 Bake slice about 45 minutes. Cool in pan.
4 Drizzle slice with melted chocolate; refrigerate until set before cutting.

preparation time 15 minutes
cooking time 45 minutes (plus cooling and refrigeration time) **makes** 16

Lemon meringue slice

90g butter, softened
2 tablespoons caster sugar
1 egg
1 cup (150g) plain flour
¼ cup (80g) apricot jam
lemon topping
2 eggs
2 egg yolks
½ cup (110g) caster sugar
300ml cream
1 tablespoon finely grated lemon rind
2 tablespoons lemon juice
meringue
3 egg whites
¾ cup (165g) caster sugar

1 Preheat oven to 200°C/180°C fan-forced. Grease 19cm x 29cm slice pan; line base with baking paper, extending paper 5cm over long sides.
2 Beat butter, sugar and egg in small bowl with electric mixer until pale in colour; stir in sifted flour, in two batches. Press dough over base of pan; prick dough all over with a fork.
3 Bake base about 15 minutes or until browned lightly. Cool 20 minutes; spread base with jam.
4 Reduce oven temperature to 170°C/150°C fan-forced.
5 Make lemon topping; pour over base. Bake about 35 minutes or until set; cool 20 minutes. Roughen surface of topping with fork.
6 Increase oven temperature to 220°C/200°C fan-forced.
7 Make meringue; spread evenly over topping.
8 Bake slice 3 minutes or until browned lightly. Cool in pan 20 minutes before cutting.
lemon topping Whisk ingredients together in medium bowl until combined.
meringue Beat egg whites in small bowl with electric mixer until soft peaks form; gradually add sugar, beating until dissolved between additions.

preparation time 20 minutes
cooking time 1 hour (plus cooling time) **makes** 16

Date squares

1¼ cups (185g) white plain flour
1¼ cups (200g) wholemeal plain flour
200g butter, chopped
½ cup (110g) caster sugar
1 egg, beaten lightly
1 tablespoon water, approximately
1 tablespoon milk
1 tablespoon raw sugar
2 teaspoons caster sugar, extra
apple date filling
1 medium apple (150g), peeled, sliced finely
1½ cups (225g) seeded dried dates, chopped coarsely
½ cup (125ml) water

1 Make apple date filling.
2 Preheat oven to 200°C/180°C fan-forced. Grease 25cm x 30cm swiss roll pan; line base with baking paper, extending paper 5cm over long sides.
3 Sift flours into large bowl, return husks from wholemeal flour to bowl; rub in butter with fingertips, stir in caster sugar. Add egg and enough water to mix to a firm dough. Knead on floured surface until smooth, cover; refrigerate 30 minutes.
4 Roll out half of the dough until large enough to cover base of pan; spread with cold apple date filling. Roll out remaining dough until large enough to cover filling; brush with milk, sprinkle with raw sugar.
5 Bake slice about 25 minutes. Cool in pan before cutting. Sprinkle with extra caster sugar.
apple date filling Place ingredients in small saucepan; simmer, covered, about 5 minutes or until pulpy. Blend or process mixture until smooth; cool.

preparation time 30 minutes (plus refrigeration time)
cooking time 30 minutes (plus cooling time) **makes** 16
tip This slice can be stored in an airtight container for up to 1 week.

Nanaimo bars

This slice originated in the city of Nanaimo, BC, Canada. According to local legend, a Nanaimo housewife entered and won a magazine contest with her chocolate squares recipe, using the title 'Nanaimo bars'.

185g butter, chopped
100g dark eating chocolate, chopped coarsely
1 egg
2 cups (200g) wheatmeal biscuit crumbs
1 cup (80g) desiccated coconut
⅔ cup (80g) finely chopped pecans
filling
60g butter, softened
1 teaspoon vanilla extract
2 cups (320g) icing sugar
2 tablespoons custard powder
¼ cup (60ml) milk
topping
30g dark eating chocolate
15g butter

1 Grease 19cm x 29cm slice pan; line base with baking paper, extending paper 5cm over long sides.
2 Make filling.
3 Melt butter and chocolate in medium saucepan over low heat; remove from heat, stir in egg. Stir in biscuit crumbs, coconut and nuts. Press mixture firmly over base of pan. Spread evenly with filling.
4 Refrigerate slice until firm.
5 Make topping.
6 Drizzle slice with topping; refrigerate 3 hours or overnight until set. Cut into pieces before serving.
filling Beat butter and extract in small bowl with electric mixer until as white as possible; gradually beat in sifted icing sugar and custard powder, then milk.
topping Melt chocolate and butter in small heatproof bowl over hot water.

preparation time 45 minutes (plus refrigeration time) **makes** 16
tip This slice can be stored, covered, in the refrigerator for up to 2 weeks.

Cranberry and pistachio muesli slice

125g butter, chopped coarsely
⅓ cup (75g) firmly packed brown sugar
2 tablespoons honey
1½ cups (135g) rolled oats
½ cup (75g) self-raising flour
1 cup (130g) dried cranberries
1 cup (140g) roasted pistachios, chopped coarsely

1 Preheat oven to 180°C/160°C fan-forced. Grease 20cm x 30cm lamington pan; line base with baking paper, extending paper 5cm over long sides.
2 Stir butter, sugar and honey in medium saucepan over medium heat without boiling until sugar is dissolved. Stir in remaining ingredients. Press mixture firmly into pan.
3 Bake slice about 20 minutes. Cool in pan before cutting.

preparation time 20 minutes
cooking time 20 minutes (plus cooling time) **makes** 30

Apricot choc-chip muesli bars

125g butter, chopped
½ cup (110g) firmly packed brown sugar
1 tablespoon honey
2¼ cups (200g) rolled oats
¼ cup (40g) sunflower kernels
¼ cup (20g) desiccated coconut
½ teaspoon ground cinnamon
½ cup (75g) chopped dried apricots
2 tablespoons dark Choc Bits

1 Preheat oven to 160°C/140°C fan-forced. Grease 20cm x 30cm lamington pan; line base with baking paper, extending paper 5cm over long sides.
2 Stir butter, sugar and honey in medium saucepan over low heat until sugar is dissolved. Transfer mixture to medium bowl; stir in oats, sunflower kernels, coconut, cinnamon and apricots. Press mixture into pan; sprinkle with Choc Bits.
3 Bake muesli bars about 30 minutes or until browned lightly. Cut into pieces while still warm; cool in pan.

preparation time 15 minutes
cooking time 30 minutes (plus cooling time) **makes** 8
tip This slice can be stored in an airtight container for up to 1 week.

Raspberry coconut slice

90g butter, softened
½ cup (110g) caster sugar
1 egg
¼ cup (35g) self-raising flour
⅔ cup (100g) plain flour
1 tablespoon custard powder
⅔ cup (220g) raspberry jam
coconut topping
2 cups (160g) desiccated coconut
¼ cup (55g) caster sugar
2 eggs, beaten lightly

1 Preheat oven to 180°C/160°C fan-forced. Grease 20cm x 30cm lamington pan; line base with baking paper, extending paper 5cm over long sides.
2 Beat butter, sugar and egg in small bowl with electric mixer until light and fluffy. Transfer to medium bowl; stir in sifted flours and custard powder. Spread dough onto base of pan; spread with jam.
3 Make coconut topping; sprinkle topping over jam.
4 Bake slice about 40 minutes. Cool in pan before cutting.
coconut topping Combine ingredients in small bowl.

variation
pistachio and marmalade Replace raspberry jam with ⅔ cup marmalade. For topping, combine 1½ cups desiccated coconut, ½ cup finely chopped unsalted pistachios, ¼ cup caster sugar, 2 eggs and 1 teaspoon finely grated orange rind in small bowl.

preparation time 25 minutes (plus cooling time)
cooking time 40 minutes **makes** 20
tip This slice can be stored in an airtight container for up to 1 week.

Vanilla slice

You need approximately 3 passionfruit for this recipe.

2 sheets ready-rolled puff pastry
½ cup (110g) caster sugar
½ cup (75g) cornflour
¼ cup (30g) custard powder
2½ cups (625ml) milk
30g butter
1 egg yolk
1 teaspoon vanilla extract
¾ cup (180ml) thickened cream
passionfruit icing
1½ cups (240g) icing sugar
1 teaspoon soft butter
¼ cup (60ml) passionfruit pulp

1 Preheat oven to 240°C/220°C fan-forced. Grease deep 23cm-square cake pan; line base with foil, extending foil 10cm over two opposite sides.
2 Place each pastry sheet on a separate greased oven tray; bake about 15 minutes, cool. Flatten pastry with hand; place one pastry sheet in cake pan, trim to fit if necessary.
3 Meanwhile, combine sugar, cornflour and custard powder in medium saucepan; gradually add milk, stirring until smooth. Add butter; stir over heat until mixture boils and thickens. Simmer, stirring, 3 minutes or until custard is thick and smooth. Remove from heat; stir in egg yolk and extract. Cover surface of custard with plastic wrap; cool to room temperature.
4 Make passionfruit icing.
5 Whip cream until firm peaks form. Fold cream into custard, in two batches. Spread custard mixture over pastry in pan. Top with remaining pastry, trim to fit if necessary; press down slightly. Spread pastry with icing; refrigerate 3 hours or overnight.
passionfruit icing Place sifted icing sugar, butter and pulp in small heatproof bowl over small saucepan of simmering water; stir until icing is spreadable.

preparation time 20 minutes (plus cooling and refrigeration time)
cooking time 35 minutes **makes** 16
tip This slice can be stored, refrigerated, in an airtight container, for up to 3 days.

Marmalade almond squares

125g butter, softened, chopped
1 teaspoon almond essence
¼ cup (55g) caster sugar
1 cup (150g) plain flour
¼ cup (20g) desiccated coconut
⅓ cup (15g) flaked coconut
¼ cup (85g) marmalade, warmed
topping
90g butter, softened, chopped
2 teaspoons grated orange rind
⅓ cup (75g) caster sugar
2 eggs
1 cup (90g) desiccated coconut
1 cup (125g) almond meal

1 Preheat oven to 200°C/180°C fan-forced. Grease 19cm x 29cm slice pan; line base with baking paper, extending paper 5cm over long sides.

2 Beat butter, essence and sugar in small bowl with electric mixer until smooth; stir in flour and desiccated coconut. Press mixture into pan.

3 Bake slice about 15 minutes or until browned lightly.

4 Meanwhile, make topping.

5 Reduce oven to 180°C/160°C fan-forced.

6 Spread hot slice with topping; sprinkle with flaked coconut.

7 Bake about 20 minutes or until firm. Brush hot slice with marmalade; cool in pan before cutting.

topping Beat butter, rind and sugar in small bowl with electric mixer until smooth; add eggs, beat until combined (mixture will look curdled at this stage). Stir in coconut and almond meal.

preparation time 30 minutes
cooking time 35 minutes (plus cooling time) **makes** 18
tip This slice can be stored, covered, in refrigerator for up to 1 week.

Chewy chocolate slice

125g butter, melted
1 cup (220g) firmly packed brown sugar
1 egg, beaten lightly
1 teaspoon vanilla extract
½ cup (75g) plain flour
¼ cup (35g) self-raising flour
2 tablespoons cocoa powder
½ cup (45g) desiccated coconut
1 tablespoon desiccated coconut, extra
chocolate icing
1 cup (160g) icing sugar
2 tablespoons cocoa powder
10g butter, melted
1½ tablespoons hot water, approximately

1 Preheat oven to 180°C/160°C fan-forced. Grease 19cm x 29cm slice pan; line base with baking paper, extending paper 5cm over long sides.
2 Combine butter, sugar, egg and extract in medium bowl. Stir in sifted flours and cocoa powder, then coconut. Spread mixture over base of pan.
3 Bake slice about 30 minutes or until firm.
4 Meanwhile, make chocolate icing.
5 Spread hot slice with chocolate icing; sprinkle with extra coconut. Cool in pan before cutting.
chocolate icing Sift icing sugar and cocoa powder into medium bowl, stir in combined butter and water until spreadable.

preparation time 20 minutes
cooking time 30 minutes (plus cooling time) **makes** 12
tip This slice can be stored in an airtight container for up to 1 week.

Chocolate and peanut butter swirl

360g white eating chocolate, chopped coarsely
½ cup (140g) smooth peanut butter
400g dark eating chocolate, chopped coarsely

1 Grease 20cm x 30cm lamington pan; line base with baking paper, extending paper 5cm above long sides.
2 Stir white chocolate in small heatproof bowl over small saucepan of simmering water until smooth; cool 5 minutes. Add peanut butter; stir until smooth.
3 Stir dark chocolate in small heatproof bowl over small saucepan of simmering water until smooth; cool slightly.
4 Drop alternate spoonfuls of white chocolate mixture and dark chocolate into pan. Gently shake pan to level mixture; pull a skewer backwards and forwards through mixtures several times for a marbled effect.
5 Stand slice at room temperature about 2 hours or until set. Cut into small pieces.

preparation time 15 minutes
cooking time 10 minutes **makes** about 72

Chocolate fudge brownies

150g butter, chopped
300g dark eating chocolate, chopped
1½ cups (330g) firmly packed brown sugar
3 eggs
1 teaspoon vanilla extract
¾ cup (110g) plain flour
¾ cup (140g) dark Choc Bits
½ cup (120g) sour cream
¾ cup (110g) roasted macadamias, chopped coarsely

1 Preheat oven to 180°C/160°C fan-forced. Grease 19cm x 29cm slice pan; line base with baking paper, extending paper 5cm over long sides.
2 Stir butter and dark chocolate in medium saucepan over low heat until smooth. Cool 10 minutes.
3 Stir sugar, eggs and extract into chocolate mixture, then sifted flour, Choc Bits, sour cream and nuts. Spread mixture into pan.
4 Bake brownies 40 minutes. Cover pan with foil; bake further 20 minutes. Cool in pan before cutting. Dust with sifted cocoa powder, if you like.

preparation time 20 minutes
cooking time 1 hour 5 minutes (plus cooling time) **makes** 20

Apple and prune slice

4 medium apples (600g)
¾ cup (135g) coarsely chopped seeded prunes
2½ cups (625ml) water
½ teaspoon ground cinnamon
½ teaspoon ground nutmeg
2 tablespoons hazelnut meal
2 sheets ready-rolled shortcrust pastry
1 tablespoon caster sugar

1 Peel and core apples; slice thinly. Place apples, prunes and the water in medium saucepan; bring to the boil. Reduce heat; simmer, covered, 10 minutes or until apples are just tender. Drain well; cool 15 minutes.
2 Combine spices and hazelnut meal in medium bowl; gently stir in apple mixture.
3 Preheat oven to 200°C/180°C fan-forced. Grease 20cm x 30cm lamington pan; line base with baking paper.
4 Roll one pastry sheet large enough to cover base of pan; place in pan, trim edges. Cover pastry with baking paper, fill with dried beans or rice; bake 15 minutes. Remove paper and beans; bake further 5 minutes. Spread apple mixture over pastry.
5 Roll remaining pastry sheet large enough to fit pan; place over apple filling. Brush pastry with a little water, sprinkle with sugar; score pastry in crosshatch pattern.
6 Bake slice about 45 minutes. Cool in pan before cutting.

preparation time 20 minutes
cooking time 1 hour 10 minutes (plus cooling time) **makes** 24

White chocolate, nut and berry blondies

125g butter, chopped coarsely
300g white eating chocolate, chopped coarsely
¾ cup (165g) caster sugar
2 eggs
¾ cup (110g) plain flour
½ cup (75g) self-raising flour
½ cup (75g) coarsely chopped roasted macadamias
150g fresh or frozen raspberries

1 Preheat oven to 180°C/160°C fan-forced. Grease 23cm-square slab cake pan; line base with baking paper, extending paper 5cm over two opposite sides.
2 Stir butter and two-thirds of the chocolate in medium saucepan over low heat until smooth. Cool 10 minutes.
3 Stir sugar and eggs into chocolate mixture, then sifted flours, remaining chocolate, nuts and berries. Spread mixture into pan.
4 Bake blondies about 40 minutes. Cool in pan before cutting. Dust with sifted icing sugar, if you like.

preparation time 20 minutes
cooking time 45 minutes (plus cooling time) **makes** 25

Pepita and sesame slice

90g butter, softened
1 teaspoon grated lemon rind
2 tablespoons caster sugar
1 egg
⅔ cup (100g) white plain flour
½ cup (80g) wholemeal plain flour
½ cup (80g) unsalted pepitas, chopped coarsely
¼ cup (80g) apricot jam
2 tablespoons sesame seeds, toasted

1 Preheat oven to 200°C/180°C fan-forced. Grease 23cm-square slab pan; line base with baking paper, extending paper 5cm over two opposite sides.
2 Beat butter, rind, sugar and egg in small bowl with electric mixer until light and fluffy. Stir in sifted flours and pepitas. Press mixture evenly into pan. Spread slice with jam; sprinkle with seeds.
3 Bake slice about 20 minutes or until browned lightly. Cool in pan before cutting.

preparation time 20 minutes
cooking time 20 minutes (plus cooling time) **makes** 16
tip This slice can be stored in an airtight container for up to 1 week.

Dutch ginger and almond slice

1¾ cups (255g) plain flour
1 cup (220g) caster sugar
⅔ cup (150g) coarsely chopped glacé ginger
½ cup (80g) blanched almonds, chopped coarsely
1 egg
185g butter, melted
2 teaspoons icing sugar

1 Preheat oven to 180°C/160°C fan-forced. Grease 20cm x 30cm lamington pan; line base with baking paper, extending paper 5cm over long sides.
2 Combine sifted flour, sugar, ginger, nuts and egg in medium bowl; stir in butter. Press mixture into pan.
3 Bake slice about 35 minutes. Stand slice in pan 10 minutes; transfer to wire rack to cool. Cut into squares; dust with sifted icing sugar.

preparation time 15 minutes
cooking time 35 minutes (plus standing time) **makes** 20
tip Crystallised ginger can be substituted for glacé ginger if rinsed with warm water and dried before use.

Caramel and chocolate slice

½ cup (75g) plain flour
½ cup (75g) self-raising flour
1 cup (90g) rolled oats
¾ cup (165g) firmly packed brown sugar
150g butter, melted
125g dark eating chocolate, chopped coarsely
½ cup (55g) coarsely chopped walnuts
¼ cup (35g) plain flour, extra
½ cup (125ml) caramel topping

1 Preheat oven to 180°C/160°C fan-forced. Grease 19cm x 29cm slice pan; line base with baking paper, extending paper 5cm over long sides.
2 Combine flours, oats and sugar in medium bowl; stir in butter. Press half the mixture into base of pan.
3 Bake base 10 minutes. Remove from oven; sprinkle with chocolate and nuts.
4 Blend extra flour and caramel topping in small bowl; drizzle evenly over chocolate and nuts. Sprinkle with remaining oat mixture.
5 Bake slice further 15 minutes. Cool in pan before cutting.

preparation time 20 minutes
cooking time 25 minutes (plus cooling time) **makes** 15
tip We used a thick, caramel-flavoured ice-cream topping in this recipe.

Hazelnut brownies

125g butter
200g dark eating chocolate, chopped coarsely
½ cup (110g) caster sugar
2 eggs, beaten lightly
1¼ cups (185g) plain flour
½ cup (70g) roasted hazelnuts, chopped coarsely
1 cup (190g) white Choc Bits

1 Preheat oven to 180°C/160°C fan-forced. Grease deep 19cm-square cake pan; line base with baking paper, extending paper 5cm above two opposite sides.
2 Stir butter and chocolate in medium saucepan over low heat until smooth. Stir in sugar; cook, stirring, 5 minutes. Cool 10 minutes.
3 Stir in egg and sifted flour, then nuts and Choc Bits. Spread mixture into pan.
4 Bake brownies about 30 minutes. Cool in pan before cutting.
Dust with icing sugar, if you like.

preparation time 15 minutes
cooking time 25 minutes **makes** 12

Chocolate caramel slice

½ cup (75g) plain flour
½ cup (75g) self-raising flour
1 cup (80g) desiccated coconut
1 cup (220g) firmly packed brown sugar
125g butter, melted
caramel filling
395g can sweetened condensed milk
30g butter
2 tablespoons golden syrup
chocolate topping
200g dark eating chocolate, chopped coarsely
2 teaspoons vegetable oil

1 Preheat oven to 180°C/160°C fan-forced. Grease 20cm x 30cm lamington pan; line base with baking paper, extending paper 5cm over long sides.
2 Combine sifted flours, coconut, sugar and butter in medium bowl; press mixture evenly over base of pan. Bake about 15 minutes or until browned lightly.
3 Meanwhile, make caramel filling.
4 Pour filling over base; bake 10 minutes. Cool.
5 Meanwhile, make chocolate topping.
6 Pour warm topping over caramel. Refrigerate 3 hours or overnight.
caramel filling Stir ingredients in small saucepan over medium heat about 15 minutes or until golden brown.
chocolate topping Stir ingredients in small heatproof bowl over small saucepan of simmering water until chocolate melts and is smooth.

variations
mocha filling Dissolve 2 teaspoons instant coffee granules in 1 tablespoon hot water; add to the condensed milk mixture with 2 tablespoons coffee-flavoured liqueur. Cook as in step 4.
white chocolate topping Replace dark eating chocolate with 180g white eating chocolate.

preparation time 20 minutes
cooking time 25 minutes (plus refrigeration time) **makes** 16
tip This slice can be stored, in an airtight container, in the refrigerator for up to 4 days.

No-bake chocolate slice

200g packet white marshmallows
1 tablespoon water
90g butter, chopped
200g dark eating chocolate, chopped coarsely
125g plain sweet biscuits, chopped coarsely
½ cup (125g) halved glacé cherries
½ cup (75g) roasted hazelnuts
½ cup (50g) walnuts
200g dark eating chocolate, melted, extra
60g butter, melted, extra

1 Grease two 8cm x 25cm bar pans; line bases with baking paper,
extending 5cm above long sides.
2 Stir marshmallows, the water and butter in medium saucepan
constantly over low heat until marshmallows are melted. Remove pan
from heat; stir in chocolate until melted.
3 Add biscuits, cherries and nuts to marshmallow mixture; stir gently
until ingredients are combined. Spread mixture evenly between pans
(do not crush biscuits). Cover; refrigerate 1 hour.
4 Combine extra chocolate and extra butter; spread mixture evenly over
slices. Refrigerate 1 hour or until firm. Remove slices from pans. Peel
away paper; cut each into 12 pieces.

preparation time 20 minutes (plus refrigeration time)
cooking time 5 minutes **makes** 24
tips This slice can be stored, covered, in the refrigerator for up to 1 week.
Pecans can be used instead of walnuts, if you like.

Tangy lemon squares

125g butter, softened
¼ cup (40g) icing sugar
1¼ cups (185g) plain flour
3 eggs
1 cup (220g) caster sugar
2 teaspoons finely grated lemon rind
½ cup (125ml) lemon juice

1 Preheat oven to 180°C/160°C fan-forced. Grease 23cm-square slab pan; line base with baking paper, extending paper 5cm above two opposite sides.
2 Beat butter and icing sugar in small bowl with electric mixer until smooth. Stir in 1 cup (150g) of the flour. Press mixture over base of pan.
3 Bake base about 15 minutes or until browned lightly.
4 Meanwhile, whisk eggs, caster sugar, remaining flour, rind and juice in bowl until combined; pour over hot base.
5 Bake slice further 20 minutes or until firm. Cool in pan, on wire rack, before cutting. Dust with extra sifted icing sugar, if you like.

preparation time 20 minutes
cooking time 35 minutes (plus cooling time) **makes** 16
tips Look for lemons that are bright and heavy – they have more juice and flavour. This slice can be stored, covered, in the refrigerator for up to 3 days.

Cashew ginger squares

125g butter, softened
¼ cup (55g) caster sugar
1 cup (150g) self-raising flour
1 teaspoon ground ginger
topping
½ cup (80g) icing sugar
60g butter
2 tablespoons golden syrup
1 cup (150g) unsalted roasted cashews, chopped coarsely
¼ cup (50g) finely chopped glacé ginger

1 Preheat oven to 180°C/160°C fan-forced. Grease 20cm x 30cm lamington pan; line base with baking paper, extending paper 5cm over long sides.
2 Beat butter and sugar in small bowl with electric mixer until light and fluffy; stir in sifted flour and ginger. Spread mixture over base of pan.
3 Bake base about 20 minutes or until browned lightly; cool in pan.
4 Meanwhile, make topping; spread hot topping over cold base. Cool.
topping Stir sifted icing sugar, butter and syrup in small saucepan over heat until butter is melted. Stir in nuts and ginger.

preparation time 20 minutes
cooking time 20 minutes **makes** 30
tip This slice can be stored, covered, in the refrigerator for up to 1 week.

Hedgehog slice

¾ cup (180ml) sweetened condensed milk
60g butter
125g dark eating chocolate, chopped coarsely
150g plain sweet biscuits
⅓ cup (45g) unsalted roasted peanuts
⅓ cup (55g) sultanas

1 Grease 8cm x 26cm bar pan; line base with baking paper, extending paper 5cm over long sides.
2 Stir condensed milk and butter in small saucepan over low heat until smooth. Remove from heat; stir in chocolate until smooth.
3 Break biscuits into small pieces; place in large bowl with nuts and sultanas. Add chocolate mixture; stir to combine.
4 Spread mixture into pan. Cover; refrigerate about 4 hours or until firm. Remove from pan; cut into slices.

preparation time 10 minutes (plus refrigeration time)
cooking time 5 minutes **makes** 12
tip This slice can be stored in an airtight container for up to 1 week.

Triple choc brownies

125g butter, chopped coarsely
200g dark eating chocolate, chopped coarsely
½ cup (110g) caster sugar
2 eggs
1¼ cups (185g) plain flour
150g white eating chocolate, chopped coarsely
100g milk eating chocolate, chopped coarsely

1 Preheat oven to 180°C/160°C fan-forced. Grease deep 19cm-square cake pan; line base with baking paper, extending paper 5cm over two opposite sides.
2 Stir butter and dark chocolate in medium saucepan over low heat until smooth. Cool 10 minutes.
3 Stir sugar and eggs into chocolate mixture, then sifted flour and white and milk chocolates. Spread mixture into pan.
4 Bake brownies about 35 minutes. Cool in pan before cutting.

preparation time 20 minutes
cooking time 40 minutes (plus cooling time) **makes** 16

Fruity white chocolate bars

⅔ cup (90g) slivered almonds
1¼ cups (210g) brazil nuts, chopped coarsely
1½ cups (135g) desiccated coconut
1 cup (150g) chopped dried apricots
1 cup (150g) dried currants
¼ cup (35g) plain flour
1⅔ cup (250g) white chocolate Melts, melted
½ cup (160g) apricot jam, warmed
½ cup (180g) honey

1 Preheat oven to 160°C/140°C fan-forced. Grease 19cm x 29cm slice pan; line base with baking paper, extending paper 5cm over long sides.
2 Combine nuts, coconut, fruit and flour in large bowl. Stir in combined hot melted chocolate, sieved jam and honey. Spread mixture into pan.
3 Bake slice about 45 minutes. Cool in pan before cutting.

preparation time 15 minutes
cooking time 45 minutes (plus cooling time) **makes** 24
tip This slice can be stored, covered, in the refrigerator for up to 1 week.

puddings

Lemon delicious puddings

125g butter, melted
2 teaspoons finely grated lemon rind
1½ cups (330g) caster sugar
3 eggs, separated
½ cup (75g) self-raising flour
⅓ cup (80ml) lemon juice
1⅓ cups (330ml) milk

1 Preheat oven to 180°C/160°C fan-forced. Grease six 1-cup (250ml) ovenproof dishes.
2 Combine butter, rind, sugar and yolks in large bowl. Stir in sifted flour then juice. Gradually stir in milk; mixture should be smooth and runny.
3 Beat egg whites in small bowl with electric mixer until soft peaks form; fold into lemon mixture, in two batches.
4 Place ovenproof dishes in large baking dish; divide lemon mixture among dishes. Add enough boiling water to baking dish to come halfway up sides of ovenproof dishes.
5 Bake puddings about 45 minutes.

preparation time 20 minutes
cooking time 45 minutes **serves** 6

College pudding

⅓ cup (110g) raspberry jam
1 egg
½ cup (110g) caster sugar
1 cup (150g) self-raising flour
½ cup (125ml) milk
25g butter, melted
1 tablespoon boiling water
1 teaspoon vanilla extract

1 Grease four 1-cup (250ml) metal moulds; divide jam among moulds.
2 Beat egg and sugar in small bowl with electric mixer until thick and creamy. Fold in sifted flour and milk, in two batches; fold in combined butter, the water and extract.
3 Spoon pudding mixture over jam. Cover each mould with pleated baking paper and foil (to allow puddings to expand as they cook); secure with kitchen string.
4 Place puddings in large saucepan with enough boiling water to come halfway up sides of moulds. Cover pan with tight-fitting lid; boil 25 minutes, replenishing water as necessary to maintain level. Stand puddings 5 minutes before turning onto serving plates. Serve with cream, if you like.

variation
golden syrup Replace the raspberry jam with ⅓ cup golden syrup.

preparation time 15 minutes
cooking time 25 minutes **serves** 4

371

Ginger sticky date pudding

1 cup (140g) seeded dried dates
¼ cup (55g) glacé ginger
1 teaspoon bicarbonate of soda
1 cup (250ml) boiling water
50g butter, chopped
½ cup (110g) firmly packed brown sugar
2 eggs
1 cup (150g) self-raising flour
1 teaspoon ground ginger
butterscotch sauce
300ml cream
¾ cup (165g) firmly packed brown sugar
75g butter, chopped

1 Preheat oven to 200°C/180°C fan-forced. Grease deep 20cm-round cake pan; line base with baking paper.
2 Place dates, ginger, soda and the water in food processor; stand 5 minutes. Add butter and sugar, then process until mixture is almost smooth. Add eggs, flour and ginger; process until combined. Pour mixture into pan.
3 Bake pudding about 45 minutes. Stand 10 minutes before turning onto serving plate.
4 Meanwhile, make butterscotch sauce.
5 Serve pudding warm with sauce.
butterscotch sauce Stir ingredients in medium saucepan over low heat until smooth.

preparation time 10 minutes
cooking time 45 minutes **serves** 8

Steamed ginger pudding

60g butter
¼ cup (90g) golden syrup
½ teaspoon bicarbonate of soda
1 cup (150g) self-raising flour
2 teaspoons ground ginger
½ cup (125ml) milk
1 egg
syrup
⅓ cup (115g) golden syrup
2 tablespoons water
30g butter

1 Grease 1.25-litre (5-cup) pudding steamer.
2 Stir butter and syrup in small saucepan over low heat until smooth. Remove from heat, stir in soda. Transfer mixture to medium bowl; stir in sifted dry ingredients, then combined milk and egg, in two batches.
3 Spread mixture into steamer. Cover with pleated baking paper and foil (to allow pudding to expand as it cooks); secure with lid.
4 Place pudding steamer in large saucepan with enough boiling water to come halfway up side of steamer; cover pan with tight-fitting lid. Boil 1 hour, replenishing water as necessary to maintain level. Stand pudding 5 minutes before turning onto plate.
5 Meanwhile, make syrup.
6 Serve pudding topped with syrup and cream, if you like.
syrup Stir ingredients in small saucepan over heat until smooth; bring to the boil. Reduce heat; simmer, uncovered, 2 minutes.

preparation time 15 minutes
cooking time 1 hour **serves** 6

375

Sago plum puddings with orange cream

Sago, also known as seed or pearl tapioca, comes from the sago palm and is used in soups and desserts, and as a thickening agent.

⅔ cup (130g) sago
2 cups (500ml) water
1 teaspoon bicarbonate of soda
250g butter, softened
2 teaspoons vanilla extract
1 cup (220g) caster sugar
1 egg
½ cup (75g) plain flour
½ teaspoon bicarbonate of soda, extra
2 cups (140g) stale breadcrumbs
2 cups (320g) sultanas
orange cream
2 teaspoons finely grated orange rind
1 tablespoon orange-flavoured liqueur
1 tablespoon icing sugar
300ml thickened cream

1 Combine sago, the water and soda in medium bowl, cover; stand overnight.
2 Preheat oven to 180°C/160°C fan-forced. Grease eight ¾-cup (180ml) ovenproof moulds.
3 Beat butter, extract, sugar and egg in small bowl with electric mixer until light and fluffy. Stir in combined sifted flour and extra soda, sago mixture, breadcrumbs and sultanas.
4 Divide mixture among moulds; cover tightly with foil. Place moulds in baking dish; pour enough boiling water into baking dish to come halfway up sides of moulds.
5 Bake puddings about 3 hours, replenishing water as necessary to maintain level.
6 Make orange cream.
7 Turn puddings into serving bowls; serve with orange cream.
orange cream Beat ingredients in small bowl with electric mixer until soft peaks form.
preparation time 10 minutes (plus standing time)
cooking time 3 hours **serves** 8
tip You can use Cointreau, Grand Marnier, Curaçao or any other orange-flavoured liqueur in this recipe.

Date and butterscotch self-saucing pudding

1 cup (150g) self-raising flour
½ cup (110g) firmly packed brown sugar
20g butter, melted
½ cup (125ml) milk
½ cup (70g) finely chopped seeded dried dates
caramel sauce
½ cup (110g) firmly packed brown sugar
1¾ cups (430ml) boiling water
50g butter

1 Preheat oven to 180°C/160°C fan-forced. Grease 2-litre (8-cup) shallow ovenproof dish.
2 Combine flour, sugar, butter, milk and dates in medium bowl. Spread mixture into dish.
3 Make caramel sauce; slowly pour sauce over the back of a spoon onto pudding mixture.
4 Bake pudding 45 minutes or until centre is firm. Stand 5 minutes before serving. Serve with cream, if you like.
caramel sauce Stir ingredients in medium heatproof jug until sugar is dissolved.

preparation time 20 minutes
cooking time 45 minutes **serves** 6

Chocolate self-saucing pudding

60g butter
½ cup (125ml) milk
½ teaspoon vanilla extract
¾ cup (165g) caster sugar
1 cup (150g) self-raising flour
1 tablespoon cocoa powder
¾ cup (165g) firmly packed brown sugar
1 tablespoon cocoa powder, extra
2 cups (500ml) boiling water

1 Preheat oven to 180°C/160°C fan-forced. Grease 1.5-litre (6-cup) ovenproof dish.
2 Stir butter and milk in medium saucepan over heat until butter is melted. Remove from heat; stir in extract and caster sugar, then sifted flour and cocoa. Spread mixture into dish.
3 Sift brown sugar and extra cocoa over mixture; slowly pour the boiling water over the back of a spoon onto pudding mixture.
4 Bake pudding 40 minutes or until centre is firm. Stand 5 minutes before serving. Serve with cream, if you like.

preparation time 20 minutes
cooking time 45 minutes **serves** 6

Mocha, pear and nut self-saucing puddings

100g dark eating chocolate, chopped
150g butter
⅔ cup (160ml) milk
1½ tablespoons instant coffee granules
⅔ cup (70g) hazelnut meal
¾ cup (165g) firmly packed brown sugar
1 cup (150g) self-raising flour
1 egg
2 medium pears (460g), sliced thinly
1¾ cups (430ml) water
¾ cup (165g) firmly packed brown sugar, extra
½ cup (50g) cocoa powder

1 Preheat oven to 180°C/160°C fan-forced. Grease eight 1¼-cup (310ml) ovenproof dishes.
2 Stir chocolate, 50g of the butter, milk and coffee in small saucepan over low heat until smooth. Transfer mixture to large bowl; stir in hazelnut meal and sugar, then sifted flour and egg.
3 Place pear slices, slightly overlapping, in dishes; top with chocolate mixture.
4 Stir the water, extra sugar, sifted cocoa and remaining butter in small saucepan over low heat until smooth; slowly pour cocoa mixture over the back of a spoon onto pudding mixture.
5 Bake puddings about 30 minutes or until centre is firm. Stand 5 minutes before serving. Serve with cream, if you like.

preparation time 35 minutes
cooking time 35 minutes **serves** 8
tip This pudding can also be made in a shallow 2.5-litre (10-cup) ovenproof dish; bake about 45 minutes.

Coffee and pecan puddings with caramel sauce

¾ cup (90g) coarsely chopped roasted pecans
300ml cream
1½ cups (330g) firmly packed brown sugar
100g cold butter, chopped
125g butter, softened
1 teaspoon vanilla extract
½ cup (110g) caster sugar
2 eggs
1 cup (150g) self-raising flour
¼ cup (35g) plain flour
¼ cup (60ml) milk
1 tablespoon finely ground espresso coffee

1 Preheat oven to 180°C/160°C fan-forced. Grease six ¾-cup (180ml) metal moulds or ovenproof dishes; line bases with baking paper.
2 Divide nuts among moulds; place moulds on oven tray.
3 Stir cream, brown sugar and chopped butter in small saucepan over heat, without boiling, until sugar dissolves. Reduce heat; simmer, uncovered, without stirring, about 5 minutes or until mixture thickens slightly. Spoon 2 tablespoons of the sauce over nuts in each mould; reserve remaining sauce.
4 Beat softened butter, extract and caster sugar in small bowl with electric mixer until light and fluffy. Beat in eggs, one at a time. Stir in sifted flours, milk and coffee; divide mixture among moulds.
5 Bake puddings about 30 minutes. Stand 5 minutes before turning onto serving plates. Reheat reserved sauce; serve puddings with warm sauce and cream, if you like.

preparation time 15 minutes
cooking time 40 minutes **serves** 6
tip The caramel sauce and puddings can be made several hours ahead and reheated before serving.

glossary

allspice also known as pimento or jamaican pepper; so-named because it tastes like a combination of nutmeg, cumin, clove and cinnamon. Available whole (a dark-brown berry the size of a pea) or ground.

almonds flat, pointy-tipped nuts having a pitted brown shell enclosing a creamy white kernel which is covered by a brown skin.

blanched brown skins removed.

flaked paper-thin slices.

meal also known as ground almonds; nuts are powdered to a coarse flour texture for use in baking or as a thickening agent.

slivered small pieces cut lengthways.

vienna toffee-coated almonds.

aniseed also called anise or sweet cumin; the seeds are the fruit of an annual plant native to Greece and Egypt. Dried, they have a strong licorice flavour which is used in alcoholic drinks such as Pernod and Ouzo, cough mixtures and baking. Whole and ground seeds are available.

baking powder a raising agent consisting mainly of two parts cream of tartar to one part bicarbonate of soda (baking soda).

bicarbonate of soda also known as baking soda; a mild alkali used as a leavening agent in baking.

bran, unprocessed is the coarse outer husk of cereal grains, and can be found in health food stores and supermarkets.

brazil nuts native to South America, a triangular-shelled oily nut with an unusually tender white flesh and a mild, rich flavour. Good for eating as well as cooking, the nuts can be eaten raw or cooked, or can be ground into meal for baking.

breadcrumbs, stale crumbs made by grating, blending or processing 1- or 2-day-old bread.

butter we use salted butter unless stated otherwise; 125g is equal to 1 stick (4oz) in other recipes. Unsalted or "sweet" butter has no added salt.

buttermilk originally the term given to the slightly sour liquid left after butter was churned from cream, today it is made similarly to yogurt. Sold alongside milk products in supermarkets. Despite the implication of its name, it is low in fat.

cardamom a spice native to India and used extensively in its cuisine; can be purchased in pod, seed or ground form. Has a distinctive aromatic, sweetly rich flavour and is one of the world's most expensive spices. Used to flavour curries, rice dishes, sweet desserts and cakes.

cheese

cream commonly known as philadelphia or philly; a soft cow-milk cheese with a fat content ranging from 14 to 33 per cent.

mascarpone an Italian fresh cultured-cream product made in much the same way as yogurt. Whiteish to creamy yellow in colour, with a buttery-rich, luscious texture. Soft, creamy and spreadable, it is used in many Italian desserts and as an accompaniment to a dessert of fresh fruit.

ricotta a soft, sweet, moist, white cow-milk cheese with a low fat content (8.5 per cent) and a slightly grainy texture. Its name roughly translates as "cooked again" and refers to ricotta's manufacture from a whey that is itself a by-product of other cheese making.

cherry small, soft stone fruit varying in colour from yellow to dark red. Sweet cherries are eaten whole and in desserts while sour cherries such as the morello variety are used for jams, preserves, pies and savoury dishes.

chocolate

Choc Bits also known as chocolate chips or chocolate morsels; available in milk, white and dark chocolate. Made of cocoa liquor, cocoa butter, sugar and an emulsifier; hold their shape in baking and are ideal for decorating.

choc Melts small discs of compounded milk, white or dark chocolate ideal for melting and moulding.

dark eating also known as semi-sweet or luxury chocolate; made of a high percentage of cocoa liquor and cocoa butter, and little added sugar. Unless stated otherwise, we use dark eating chocolate in this book as it's ideal for use in desserts and cakes.

white contains no cocoa solids but derives its sweet flavour from cocoa butter. Very sensitive to heat.

chocolate-flavoured liqueur we use crème de cacao chocolate-flavoured liqueur.

chocolate hazelnut spread we use Nutella. It was originally developed when chocolate was hard to source during World War 2; hazelnuts were added to extend the chocolate supply.

cinnamon available both in the piece (called sticks or quills) and ground into powder; one of the world's most common spices, used universally as a sweet, fragrant flavouring for both sweet and savoury foods. The dried inner bark of the shoots of the Sri Lankan native cinnamon tree; much of what is sold as the real thing is in fact cassia, Chinese cinnamon, from the bark of the cassia tree. Less expensive to process than true cinnamon, it is often blended with Sri Lankan cinnamon to produce the type of "cinnamon" most commonly found in supermarkets.

cloves dried flower buds of a tropical tree; can be used whole or in ground form. They have a strong scent and taste so should be used sparingly.

cocoa powder also known as unsweetened cocoa; cocoa beans (cacao seeds) that have been fermented, roasted, shelled, ground into powder then cleared of most of the fat content. Unsweetened cocoa is used in hot chocolate drink mixtures; milk powder and sugar are added to the ground product.

coconut

desiccated concentrated, dried, unsweetened and finely shredded coconut flesh.

flaked dried flaked coconut flesh.

shredded unsweetened thin strips of dried coconut flesh.

coconut-flavoured liqueur we use Malibu coconut-flavoured liqueur.

coffee-flavoured liqueur we use either Kahlua or Tia Maria coffee-flavoured liqueur.

corella pears are miniature dessert pears with pale flesh and a sweet, mild flavour.

cornflour also known as cornstarch. Available made from corn or wheat (wheaten cornflour, gluten-free, gives a lighter texture in cakes); used as a thickening agent in cooking.

cream of tartar the acid ingredient in baking powder; added to confectionery mixtures to help prevent sugar from crystallising. Keeps frostings creamy and improves volume when beating egg whites.

custard powder instant mixture used to make pouring custard; similar to North American instant pudding mixes.

dates fruit of the date palm tree, eaten fresh or dried, on their own or in prepared dishes. About 4cm to 6cm in length, oval and plump, thin-skinned, with a honey-sweet flavour and sticky texture. Best known, perhaps, for its inclusion in sticky toffee pudding; also found in muesli and other cereals; muffins, scones and cakes; compotes and stewed fruit desserts.

dried cranberries have the same slightly sour, succulent flavour as fresh cranberries. Can usually be substituted for or with other dried fruit in most recipes. Available in most supermarkets. Also available in sweetened form.

dried currants dried tiny, almost black raisins so-named from the grape type native to Corinth, Greece; most often used in jams, jellies and sauces (the best-known of which is the English cumberland sauce). These are not the same as fresh

currants, which are the fruit of a plant in the gooseberry family.

egg we use large chicken eggs (60g) in our recipes unless stated otherwise. If a recipe calls for raw or barely cooked eggs, exercise caution if there is a salmonella problem in your area.

essences are synthetically produced substances used in small amounts to impart their respective flavours to foods. An extract is made by actually extracting the flavour from a food product. In the case of vanilla, pods are soaked, usually in alcohol, to capture the authentic flavour. Both extracts and essences will keep indefinitely if stored in a cool dark place.

figs fresh figs are best eaten in peak season, at the height of summer. Vary in skin and flesh colour according to type not ripeness: the purple-black mission or black mission fig, with pink flesh, is a rich-flavoured, good all-rounder; the thick-skinned, pale green kadota, is good canned or dried as well as fresh; the yellow smyrna has nutty-tasting flesh; and the pale olive, golden-skinned adriatic has

honey-sweet, light pink flesh. When ripe, figs should be unblemished and bursting with flesh; nectar beads at the base indicate when a fig is at its best.

flour

plain also known as all-purpose; unbleached wheat flour is the best for baking.

rice very fine, almost powdery, gluten-free flour; made from ground white rice. Used in baking, as a thickener, and in some Asian noodles and desserts.

self-raising all-purpose plain or wholemeal flour with baking powder and salt added; can be made at home with plain or wholemeal flour sifted with baking powder in the proportion of 1 cup flour to 2 teaspoons baking powder.

wholemeal also known as wholewheat flour; milled with the wheat germ so is higher in fibre and more nutritional than white flour. Available plain and self-raising.

gelatine a thickening agent. Available in sheet form, known as leaf gelatine, or as a powder. Three teaspoons of dried gelatine (8g or one sachet) is roughly equivalent to four gelatine leaves.

food colouring vegetable-based substance available in liquid, paste or gel form.

ginger

crystallised sweetened with cane sugar.

fresh also called green or root ginger; the thick gnarled root of a tropical plant. Can be kept, peeled, covered, with dry sherry in a jar and refrigerated, or frozen in an airtight container.

glacé fresh ginger root preserved in sugar syrup; crystallised ginger can be substituted if rinsed with warm water and dried before using.

ground also known as powdered ginger; used as a flavouring in cakes, pies and puddings but cannot be substituted for fresh ginger.

ginger wine a beverage that is 14 per cent alcohol by volume, has the piquant taste of fresh ginger. Available at hotels and bottle shops.

glacé cherries also known as candied cherries; boiled in heavy sugar syrup and then dried. Used in cakes, breads and sweets.

glacé fruit fruit such as pineapple, apricots, peaches and pears that are cooked in a heavy sugar syrup then dried.

golden syrup a by-product of refined sugarcane; pure maple syrup or honey can be substituted. Golden syrup and treacle (a thicker, darker syrup not unlike molasses), also known as flavour syrups, are similar sugar products made by partly breaking down sugar into its component parts and adding water. Treacle is more viscous, and has a stronger flavour and aroma than golden syrup.

hazelnuts also known as filberts; plump, grape-size, rich, sweet nut having a brown inedible skin that is removed by rubbing heated nuts together vigorously in a tea-towel.

meal is made by grounding the hazelnuts to a coarse flour texture.

hazelnut-flavoured liqueur we use frangelico.

honey the variety sold in a squeezable container is not suitable for the recipes in this book.

jam also known as preserve or conserve.

jersey caramels are a softish confectionery, caramel in colour with a white stripe in the middle. Available in supermarkets and chain stores.

kumara the polynesian name of an orange-fleshed sweet potato often confused with yam; good baked, boiled, mashed or fried similarly to other potatoes.

macadamias native to Australia; fairly large, slightly soft, buttery rich nut. Should always be stored in the fridge to prevent their high oil content turning them rancid.

maple-flavoured syrup is made from sugar cane and is also known as golden or pancake syrup. It is not a substitute for pure maple syrup.

maple syrup distilled from the sap of sugar maple trees found only in Canada and about ten states in the USA. Most often eaten with pancakes or waffles, but also used as an ingredient in baking or in preparing desserts. Maple-flavoured syrup or pancake syrup is not an adequate substitute for the real thing.

marmalade a preserve, usually based on citrus fruit.

matzo meal is available from some supermarkets and delicatessens. If you can't find it, make your own by processing matzo crackers, biscuit-like unleavened bread, found in boxes on most supermarket shelves.

milk we use full-cream homogenised milk unless stated otherwise.

skim sometimes labelled 'no-fat'; both have 0.1 per cent fat content.

sweetened condensed a canned milk product consisting of milk with more than half the water content removed and sugar added to the remaining milk.

mixed peel candied citrus peel.

mixed spice a classic mixture generally containing caraway, allspice, coriander, cumin, nutmeg and ginger, although cinnamon and other spices can be added. It is used with fruit and in cakes.

muesli also known as granola; a combination of grains (mainly oats), nuts and dried fruits.

nutmeg a strong and very pungent spice ground from the dried nut of an evergreen tree native to Indonesia. Usually found ground but the flavour is more intense from a whole nut, available from spice shops, so it's best to grate your own. Found in mixed spice mixtures.

oil

cooking spray we use a cholesterol-free cooking spray made from canola oil.

olive made from ripened olives. Extra virgin and virgin are the first and second press, respectively, of the olives and are therefore considered the best; types named "extra light" or "light" refer to taste not fat levels.

vegetable any of a number of oils sourced from plant rather than animal fats.

orange-flavoured liqueur we use either Grand Marnier (an orange-flavoured liqueur) or Cointreau (a citrus-flavoured liqueur).

pecans native to the US and now grown locally; pecans are golden brown, buttery and rich. Good in savoury as well as sweet dishes; walnuts are a good substitute.

pepitas the pale green kernels of dried pumpkin seeds; available plain or salted.

pine nuts also known as pignoli; not in fact a nut but a small, cream-coloured kernel from pine cones. They are best roasted before use to bring out the flavour.

pistachios green, delicately flavoured nuts inside hard off-white shells. Available salted or unsalted in their shells; you can also get them shelled.

polenta also known as cornmeal; a flour-like cereal made of dried corn (maize). Also the name of the dish made from it.

poppy seeds small, dried, bluish-grey seeds of the poppy plant, with a crunchy texture and a nutty flavour. Can be purchased whole or ground in most supermarkets.

quince yellow-skinned fruit with hard texture and astringent, tart taste; eaten cooked or as a preserve. Long, slow cooking makes the flesh a deep rose pink.

raisins dried sweet grapes (traditionally muscatel grapes).

ready-rolled puff pastry packaged sheets of frozen puff pastry, available from supermarkets.

rhubarb classified as a vegetable, is eaten as a fruit and therefore considered one. Leaves must be removed before cooking as they can contain traces of poison; the edible crisp, pink-red stalks are chopped and cooked.

rolled oats flattened oat grain rolled into flakes and traditionally used for porridge. Instant oats are also available, but traditional oats are best for baking.

rolled rice flattened rice grain rolled into flakes; looks similar to rolled oats.

rosewater extract made from crushed rose petals; used for its aromatic quality.

rum we prefer to use an underproof rum in baking because of its more subtle flavour; however, you can use an overproof rum and still get satisfactory results.

semolina coarsely ground flour milled from durum wheat; the flour used in making gnocchi, pasta and couscous.

sesame seeds black and white are the most common of this small oval seed, however there are also red and brown varieties. The seeds are used in cuisines the world over as an ingredient and as a condiment. Roast the seeds in a heavy-based frying pan over low heat.

sherry fortified wine consumed as an aperitif or used in cooking. Sherries differ in colour and flavour; sold as fino (light, dry), amontillado (medium sweet, dark) and oloroso (full-bodied, very dark).

sour cream thick, commercially-cultured sour cream with a minimum fat content of 35 per cent.

star anise a dried star-shaped pod whose seeds have an astringent aniseed flavour.

sugar we use coarse, granulated table sugar, also called crystal sugar, unless stated otherwise.

brown an extremely soft, fine granulated sugar retaining molasses for its characteristic colour and flavour.

caster also known as superfine or finely granulated table sugar. The fine crystals dissolve easily so it is perfect for cakes, meringues and desserts.

coffee crystal large golden-coloured crystal sugar made to enhance the flavour of coffee.

demarara small-grained golden-coloured crystal sugar.

icing also known as confectioners' sugar or powdered sugar; pulverised granulated sugar crushed together with a small amount (about 3 per cent) of cornflour.

pure icing also known as confectioners' sugar or powdered sugar.

raw natural brown granulated sugar.

treacle thick, dark syrup not unlike molasses; a by-product of sugar refining.

vanilla

bean dried, long, thin pod from a tropical golden orchid grown in central and South America and Tahiti; the minuscule black seeds inside the bean are used to impart a luscious vanilla flavour in baking and desserts. Place a whole bean in a jar of sugar to make vanilla sugar.

essence obtained from vanilla beans infused in alcohol and water.

extract obtained from vanilla beans infused in water; a non-alcoholic version of essence.

vinegar, malt made from fermented malt and beech shavings.

walnuts as well as being a good source of fibre and healthy oils, nuts contain a range of vitamins, minerals and other beneficial plant components called phytochemicals. Each type of nut has a special make-up and walnuts contain the beneficial omega-3 fatty acids, which is terrific news for people who dislike the taste of fish.

yogurt we use plain full-cream yogurt in our recipes unless stated otherwise. If we call for low-fat yogurt, we use one with a fat content of less than 0.2 per cent.

index

392

conversion chart

MEASURES

One Australian metric measuring cup holds approximately 250ml, one Australian metric tablespoon holds 20ml, one Australian metric teaspoon holds 5ml.

The difference between one country's measuring cups and another's is within a two- or three-teaspoon variance, and will not affect your cooking results.North America, New Zealand and the United Kingdom use a 15ml tablespoon.

All cup and spoon measurements are level. The most accurate way of measuring dry ingredients is to weigh them. When measuring liquids, use a clear glass or plastic jug with the metric markings.

We use large eggs with an average weight of 60g.

LIQUID MEASURES

METRIC	IMPERIAL
30ml	1 fluid oz
60ml	2 fluid oz
100ml	3 fluid oz
125ml	4 fluid oz
150ml	5 fluid oz (¼ pint/1 gill)
190ml	6 fluid oz
250ml	8 fluid oz
300ml	10 fluid oz (½ pint)
500ml	16 fluid oz
600ml	20 fluid oz (1 pint)
1000ml (1 litre)	1¾ pints

LENGTH MEASURES

METRIC	IMPERIAL
3mm	⅛in
6mm	¼in
1cm	½in
2cm	¾in
2.5cm	1in
5cm	2in
6cm	2½in
8cm	3in
10cm	4in
13cm	5in
15cm	6in
18cm	7in
20cm	8in
23cm	9in
25cm	10in
28cm	11in
30cm	12in (1ft)

DRY MEASURES

METRIC	IMPERIAL
15g	½oz
30g	1oz
60g	2oz
90g	3oz
125g	4oz (¼lb)
155g	5oz
185g	6oz
220g	7oz
250g	8oz (½lb)
280g	9oz
315g	10oz
345g	11oz
375g	12oz (¾lb)
410g	13oz
440g	14oz
470g	15oz
500g	16oz (1lb)
750g	24oz (1½lb)
1kg	32oz (2lb)

OVEN TEMPERATURES

These oven temperatures are only a guide for conventional ovens.
For fan-forced ovens, check the manufacturer's manual.

	°C (CELSIUS)	°F (FAHRENHEIT)	GAS MARK
Very slow	120	250	½
Slow	150	275 – 300	1 – 2
Moderately slow	160	325	3
Moderate	180	350 – 375	4 – 5
Moderately hot	200	400	6
Hot	220	425 – 450	7 – 8
Very hot	240	475	9

General manager Christine Whiston
Editorial director Susan Tomnay
Creative director Hieu Chi Nguyen
Art director Caryl Wiggins
Senior editor Stephanie Kistner
Food director Pamela Clark
Test Kitchen manager Belinda Farlow
Recipe consultant Louise Patniotis
Director of sales Brian Cearnes
Marketing manager Bridget Cody
Senior business analyst Rebecca Varela
Operations manager David Scotto
Production manager Victoria Jefferys
International rights enquiries Laura Bamford
lbamford@acpuk.com

ACP Books are published by ACP Magazines
a division of PBL Media Pty Limited
Publishing director, Women's lifestyle Pat Ingram
Director of sales, Women's lifestyle Lynette Phillips
Commercial manager, Women's lifestyle Seymour Cohen
Marketing director, Women's lifestyle Matthew Dominello
Public relations manager, Women's lifestyle Hannah Deveraux
Research director, Women's lifestyle Justin Stone
PBL Media, Chief Executive Officer Ian Law

Produced by ACP Books, Sydney.
Published by ACP Books, a division of ACP Magazines Ltd.
54 Park St, Sydney NSW Australia 2000. GPO Box 4088, Sydney, NSW 2001.
Phone +61 2 9282 8618 Fax +61 2 9267 9438
acpbooks@acpmagazines.com.au www.acpbooks.com.au
Printed by Toppan Printing Co., China.

Australia Distributed by Network Services, GPO Box 4088, Sydney, NSW 2001.
Phone +61 2 9282 8777 Fax +61 2 9264 3278
networkweb@networkservicescompany.com.au
United Kingdom Distributed by Australian Consolidated Press (UK),
10 Scirocco Close, Moulton Park Office Village, Northampton, NN3 6AP.
Phone +44 1604 642 200 Fax +44 1604 642 300
books@acpuk.com www.acpuk.com
New Zealand Distributed by Southern Publishers Group, 21 Newton Road, Auckland.
Phone +64 9 360 0692 Fax +64 9 360 0695 hub@spg.co.nz
South Africa Distributed by PSD Promotions, 30 Diesel Road Isando, Gauteng Johannesburg.
PO Box 1175, Isando 1600, Gauteng Johannesburg.
Phone +27 11 392 6065/6/7 Fax +27 11 392 6079/80 orders@psdprom.co.za
Canada Distributed by Publishers Group Canada
Order Desk & Customer Service 9050 Shaughnessy Street, Vancouver BC V6P 6E5
Phone (800) 663 5714 Fax (800) 565 3770 service@raincoast.com

Title: Mix/food director, Pamela Clark.
ISBN: 978-1-86396-869-0 (pbk)
Notes: Includes index
Subjects: Recipes
Other authors/contributors: Clark, Pamela
Also titled: Australian women's weekly
Dewey number: 640.2
© ACP Magazines Ltd 2009
ABN 18 053 273 546

To order books, phone 136 116 (within Australia).
Send recipe enquiries to: recipeenquiries@acpmagazines.com.au

The publishers would like to thank Mud Australia for props used in photography.

Front cover Genoise sponge, page 129
Front cover photographer Ben Dearnley
Front cover stylist Vanessa Austin
Front cover photochef Belinda Farlow
Illustrations Hannah Blackmore
Back cover photographers John Paul Urizar, Louise Lister
Back cover stylists Micheala Le Compte, Lynsey Fryers